Meeting New Friends

Second Edition

Florence M. Lindstrom

Christian Liberty Press
Arlington Heights, Illinois

Meeting New Friends, Second Edition
Copyright © 2006, 1992 by Christian Liberty Press

All rights reserved. No part of this book may be reproduced or transmitted in any form or by any means, electronic or mechanical, without written permission from the publisher. Brief quotations embodied in critical articles or reviews are permitted.

A publication of

Christian Liberty Press
502 West Euclid Avenue
Arlington Heights, IL 60004
www.christianlibertypress.com

Written by Florence M. Lindstrom
Editing and layout by Edward J. Shewan
Copyediting by Diane C. Olson and Belit M. Shewan
Cover design and layout by Bob Fine
Graphics by Edward J. Shewan and Bob Fine

All graphics were acquired from Design Pics, Inc.™ at **designpics.com**; except for photos taken by Bob Fine for the cover and copyright page, and text pages 104, 110, and 162; Corel™ image on page 55; PhotoDisc™ image on page 57 and clock image on page 134; and artwork by Chris Kou on page 25 and Vic Lockman on page 73.

"God's Gifts," by Hannah McHugh, Copyright © 2006. Used with permission.

ISBN-13: 978-1-932971-00-2
ISBN-10: 1-932971-00-9

Printed in China

Contents

Meeting New Friends

Contents

To Parents and Teachers

Meeting New Friends is for students who have learned their sounds and have begun to read words having short and long vowels, as well as the other vowel sounds. These lessons are for review and reinforcement in addition to introducing new words. Please be careful to have your student learn to read the lesson well before going on to a new story.

Each lesson is completed on one or two pages. However, it is highly recommended that your student be encouraged to study and master the Word Charts in the back of the book, working on the words of one or more charts before doing the lesson. The charts will teach the student almost 1,400 words.

Questions after the lessons are to help strengthen the student's comprehension. Work closely as you teach him to answer in complete sentences, first orally and then printing them on appropriate line paper, looking for the answers in each lesson. Grammar skills should be applied as each sentence begins with a capital letter and ends with a period.

Use good judgment as to the length of drill time that your student should spend on each chart. Be generous with encouragement and praise, perhaps rewarding him by attatching a small star by each chart as it is mastered. Your enthusiasm will be catching. Review as much as needed.

It is our hope that students will be well prepared in phonics skills to enable them to truly enjoy reading, making them eager to learn from their studies. May God bless your efforts....

> ... For the LORD gives wisdom: out of his mouth comes knowledge and understanding. He lays up sound wisdom for the righteous; he is a buckler to them that walk uprightly. (*Proverbs 2:6–7*)

The Publishers

WORDS TO KNOW: Study Chart I

Dăn	lăds(z)	căn	hănds(z)	ŏn
Săm	glăd	hăve	stănd	ĭs
hăng	săd	păl	ăs	hĭs
the(ə)	măd	ănd	făst	gō

Sam and Dan

Hang on, Dan! Hang on, Sam! The lads' hands have to hang on. Dan and Sam stand and go fast. Is Sam mad? Is Dan sad? Dan is glad to go fast. Sam is glad he can go as fast as his pal Dan.

Questions:

1. Who is Dan's pal?
2. How do they hang on?
3. Are they sad or glad?

WORDS TO KNOW: Study Chart I

Păm	păl	ĭn	rīde
Tăg	ăf′ ter(ər)	to(ū)	cär
năp	wĭll	whīte	her(ər)

Pam's Pal

Pam has a fat, white pal. Her pal is Tag. Tag is glad to have a ride in Pam's car. Pam has her hands on the car and on Tag. Pam and Tag can go fast. After Pam and Tag have had a ride, Tag will be glad to have a nap.

Questions:

1. What is the name of Pam's pal?
2. What color is Tag?
3. What did Pam and Tag ride in?

WORDS TO KNOW: Study Chart I

dăd	thănk	ĭn' to(ū)	mākes
A'(ă) lan(ə)	bŭt	sēe	Gŏd
plănt	lĭt' tle(əl)	sēed	ō' pĕns
lănd	ĭn sīde'	grōw	of(əv)

Alan and His Dad

Alan's dad has seeds in his hands. As Alan and his dad sit on the land, his dad opens a seed to see inside of it. Can a little seed grow into a plant? Dad and Alan can plant the seeds, but God makes the seeds grow into plants. Alan and his dad thank God.

Questions:

1. What does the man have in his hand?
2. What is the lad's name?
3. Can Alan make the seeds grow into plants?

Lesson 4

WORDS TO KNOW: Study Charts I, 13

Brăd	sănd	dămp	căs' tle(əl)
Mătt	grănd	nŏt	wāves
flăt	păt	plāy	bē

Brad and Matt

Brad and Matt have fun on the sand. The pals can pat the damp sand and make a grand castle.

Can the castle stand if it gets wet? As the waves pass on the castle, it will not stand. The waves will make the castle flat. Brad and Matt will not be sad. It is fun to play in the sand.

Questions:

1. Where are the boys playing?
2. What are they making with the sand?
3. What will happen if the waves pass on it?

Do You Remember?

Dan and Sam can stand and go fast. Dan is glad Sam is his pal. Sam and Dan hang on and go fast.

Pam and her fat, white pal can ride fast in the car. Pam's hand is on the car and on Tag.

Alan's dad has seeds in his hands. Can the seeds grow into plants? Only God can make the seeds grow into plants.

Brad and Matt have fun on the damp sand. The castle will not stand as waves pass on it. The waves will make the castle flat.

Questions:

1. Where are Brad and Matt playing?
2. What will make the castle flat?

WORDS TO KNOW: Study Chart 2

Bĕn	sĕt	bĕd	băck′ păck
tĕnt	lĕft	rĕd	trĭp
gĕt	bĕst	nĕxt	wĭth
lĕt	vĕst	păck	rŏd
nĕt	rĕst	păck~~e~~d(t)	făm′ i(ə) l~~y~~ (ē)

A Family Trip

Ben and his family will get packed to go west on a trip. He will pack his red vest and best cap. Ben will set his backpack next to his bed.

Dad will pack a tent in the van. He let Ben pack his rod and net. After Ben had a rest, his family left on the trip. He is glad to be with his family.

Questions:

1. Who went on a trip?
2. What did Ben put next to his bed?
3. What did Dad pack in the van?

WORDS TO KNOW: | Study Chart 2

wĕnt	stĕps	fŭn	Grănd
wĕst	lo͝ok′ out	could (o͝o)	Căn′yon(ə)
spĕnt	now(ou)	cămp	tīme
spĕnd	mŭch	bĭg	dāys(z)
lĕd	tĕn	ĭf	they(ā)

The Grand Canyon

Ben's family went west and spent a day at a big canyon. It is the Grand Canyon. Dad led his family as they went on steps to a lookout. Now they could see much of the canyon.

It is time to set up the tent and rest. It is fun to camp on the land. They will spend ten days on the trip.

Questions:

1. What is the name of this canyon?
2. Where did Dad lead his family?
3. How many days will they spend on the trip?

WORDS TO KNOW: Study Chart 2

vĕnt	pĕgs	cŏt
yĕt	slĕpt	fôr

A Bed in the Tent

See the big tent? Ben's dad has set up the tent and held it with pegs. It is next to the van. The tent has a net for a vent. Ben is glad to spend time in the tent.

Dad let Ben get in the tent and set up a cot for his bed. Ben has not slept in the tent yet. He thinks he will get his best rest.

Questions:

1. Where did Ben's dad set the tent?
2. What held the tent up?
3. What did Ben set up in the tent?

WORDS TO KNOW: Study Chart 2

wh<u>o</u>(ū)	slĭp	lĕgs	rŏcks
ĭf	dĭd	wĕt	fä' th<u>er</u>(ər)
thĭs	stĕp	māde	strēam

God Made This Big Land

See Ben's father step on the rocks. Did he get wet? He will get wet if his legs slip.

See the waves in the stream! Who made the stream and rocks? Who made this land? God made the stream and rocks. God made this big land. Ben is glad to see this big land.

Questions:

1. Who steps on the rocks?
2. What will happen if he slips?
3. Who made the stream and rocks?

Do You Remember?

Ben and his family went on a trip west. Dad packed a tent in the van. He let Ben pack his rod and net. Ben set his backpack next to his bed.

The family went to see the Grand Canyon. God made this big canyon. Dad set up the tent and the family slept in it. It was fun to camp on the land.

Ben's dad will step on the rocks. He will get wet if his legs slip. God made the stream and the rocks in this big land.

Questions:

1. What did Dad pack in the van?
2. What big canyon did the family see?
3. Who made the stream and the rocks?

WORDS TO KNOW: Study Charts 3 and 13

ăsks	glăss	stŏp	lŭnch
hĭlls(z)	fĭll	stĭll	nō
sĭt	tĭp	chĭps	sănd' wĭch
mĭlk	fĭx(ks)	lĭt' tle(əl)	thănks
pĭc' nĭc	gōes(z)	ŭp	

The Big Hills

See the big hills! Ben's family sits still as the van goes up in the hills. Will the van tip? No, it will not tip.

Mother asks Father to stop and have lunch. She will fix a picnic lunch. Ben sits with his father and mother. His father thanks God for the picnic. Ben fills his glass with milk and has chips and a sandwich. Then he has a little nap.

Questions:

1. How does Ben's family sit in the van?
2. What will Ben's mother fix?
3. What is in Ben's glass?

WORDS TO KNOW: Study Chart 3

clĭffs	bĭg′ gest(ə)	work′(ər) ers(ər)
yoū	pĭc′ ture(chər)	world(ər)
were(ər)	they(ā)	fā′ ces(səz)
dĭg	ĭm pôr′ tant(ə)	lông
drĭll	worked(ər,t)	Prĕs′(z) i(ə) dents(ə)

Men in the Hills

Can you see the faces of men in the cliffs? They are the biggest in the world. Workers had to dig and drill in the cliffs to make the big men. They worked a long time.

Did Ben and his family go up to the men on the cliffs? They did not go up to the men, but Ben's dad did get a picture. The men in the cliffs were important Presidents.

Questions:

1. What do you see on the cliffs?
2. What did the workers have to do?
3. Who were the men?

WORDS TO KNOW: Study Chart 4

c̲ome (ŭ)	hŭnt	shôre
hŏt	friĕnd	ĕv′ery̲(ē) thĭng
lŏt	mĕt	knōw
rŭn	o̲f(əv)	făm′ i̲(ə) ly̲(ē)
sŭn	shĕlls	friĕnds̲(z)

At the Shore

Ben's family has come west to the shore. Ben has met a friend. The pals like to hunt for rocks and shells. They have a lot of shells in their hands.

It is fun to sit in the hot sun. It is fun to run and hunt on the shore. They will get wet, but Mother will not get mad. They know God made the shells, rocks, and everything they see.

Questions:

1. What do the friends have in their hands?
2. How does the sun feel?
3. Will Ben and his friend get wet?

WORDS TO KNOW: Study Chart 5

Dŏn	mŭd' dy̲(ē)	lôgs̲(z)	hĭd
bŭgs	clŭmp	grăss	ănts
dŭg	stŭmp	twĭg	smĕllẹd
slŭg	skŭnk	so̲mẹ'(ə) thĭng	ōh
grŭbs̲(z)	ŭn' de̲r(ər)	sŭd' dĕn(ə) ly̲(ē)	

Hunting

Ben and his friend Don like to hunt for bugs under rocks and logs. Some grubs were under a muddy twig. A slug was in a stump. A bug hid under a clump of grass. A lot of ants had dug into a hill of sand.

Suddenly Don smelled something. It was a bad smell. It made Ben and Don run back to the tent. Oh, oh! A skunk had run past them.

Questions:

1. What was under a muddy twig?
2. What was under a clump of grass?
3. What made Ben and Don run to the tent?

Do You Remember?

Ben's mother asks his father to stop and have a picnic lunch. Ben fills his glass with milk and has chips and a sandwich.

Ben can see the big faces of men on a cliff. They are the biggest in the world. Workers had to drill and dig to make them.

Ben and his friend like to hunt for shells on the shore. They like to hunt for bugs on rocks and logs, too. They smelled the bad smell of a skunk and ran back to the tent.

They know God made the shells, rocks, and everything we can see.

Questions:

1. What did Ben have in his glass?
2. What did Ben and his friend hunt for on rocks?
3. Who made everything?

WORDS TO KNOW:

Study Chart 8

cāme	prāyed	lāte	hōme
wāy	bāke	nīne	shŏp
stāy	wāke	sāfe	hĕlps
prāy	tāke	slēep	

Glad to Be Home

Ben is glad his family came home after ten days. They went a long way. They came home late, so they did not wake up until nine. Ben was glad to sleep in his bed. They prayed to God to thank Him for the safe trip.

Ben helps take in everything from the van, and then he will play with his friends. Dad will read the big box of mail. Mother will shop and bake. They have to work, but they are glad to stay home.

Questions:

1. How long was Ben's family gone?
2. Who did they thank for the safe trip?
3. What did Ben's dad have to do?

WORDS TO KNOW: Study Chart 8

Jāke	lāke	māy	ō′ pĕn
plāne	āim	gō′ ĭng	grănd
gāve	tāil	trēe	kĭt
māke	plāce(s)	fly(ī)	to(ū) gĕ′ ther(ər)

Jake's Plane

Jake has a plane that his grandfather gave to him. It came in a kit that he had to make. He may paint the tail of the plane. He will take it to a big open place to make it fly. He will aim to keep it from going into a tree or lake.

Jake thanked his grandfather for his plane. Grandfather gave Jake help as he made it. Jake and his grandfather are dear friends. They are so glad to be together.

Questions:

1. What did Jake's grandfather give to him?
2. How will he keep it from going into a tree?
3. Who helped Jake make the plane?

WORDS TO KNOW: Study Chart 8

Kĕl′ sēy	cāke	fĭsh	won′(ə) der(ər) ful(ə)
tāme	swĭm	rāin′ y(ē)	yĕs′ ter(ər) dāy
a(ə) wāy′	from(ŭ)	what(ŭ)	

Kelsey Plays by the Lake

What a wonderful day it is! Kelsey came to the lake to play. She waves at the fish as they swim. They are not tame, and they swim away from her. She will take care in the way she plays on the rocks so she will be safe. It was a rainy day yesterday, so she did not come.

Kelsey will not stay late today. She must help her mother bake a cake.

Questions:

1. What do the fish do as Kelsey waves at them?
2. What will Kelsey and her mother bake?

WORDS TO KNOW: Study Chart 8

Dā′ vĭd	crān~~e~~	wād~~e~~	hol~~e~~
trā~~i~~l	snāk~~e~~	fly(ī)	cōōl
wā~~i~~t	rāk~~e~~	a(ə) lông′	fall(ô)

On a Trail

David and his father take a trail along a lake. They stop and wait as they see a big crane take off and fly away. It has long legs and a big bill. A snake came along a gray rock. The snake is not tame and went into a hole.

The day was cool in the fall so they will not wade in the lake. They will go home and rake leaves.

Questions:

1. What bird did they see fly away?
2. What will they do when they go home?

Do You Remember?

Ben's family came home. They went a long way on the trip. They thank God that they are safe. Ben is glad to play with his friends.

Jake made a plane that his grandfather gave to him. He will take it to a big open place to fly it. He will aim so it will not go into a lake or tree. He is so glad to have his grandfather as a friend.

Kelsey waves at fish as they swim. She will take care in the way she plays on the rocks. She will go home to help her mother bake a cake.

David and his father see a snake on the trail along a lake. They see a big crane fly away. It is a cool day, so they will not wade in the lake. It is time to go home and rake leaves.

Questions:

1. Who did Ben play with when he came home?
2. Who gave Jake his plane?
3. Who will Kelsey help to bake a cake?
4. What did David see on the trail along a lake?

WORDS TO KNOW: Study Chart 9

Pē′ ter(ər)	dēar	nēed	rŭg / put(o͝o)
ēat	ēars	fēet	kĭt′ chen(ə)
nēat	whēat	slēep′ y(ē)	drĕssed(t)
clēan	Jēan	tēeth	Păs′ tor(ər)
thrēe	tēeth	cēr′ ē al(ə)	Dēan

Time to Eat

"Wake up, Peter, wake up! You need to get up and eat. We need to work and make our home clean and neat. At three o'clock you will see a dear friend. Come, Peter, come and eat some wheat cereal."

Peter's ears did hear his mother tell him to get up. He was still sleepy, but he got up and put his feet on the rug next to his bed. He got dressed and ran to Mother in the kitchen.

Will Grandpa come? Will Aunt Jean come? Peter did not know which dear friend was coming.

He ate his wheat cereal. After he brushed his teeth, he helped Mother clean the home. Mother did not tell him the name of the friend.

At three o'clock the friend came to the home. It was Pastor Dean. He was a wonderful friend to Peter. They sat with Mother and had a cup of tea.

Questions:

1. What did Peter eat for breakfast?
2. What did they do before the friend came?
3. Who was the friend?

WORDS TO KNOW:

Study Chart 9

hēap	mēan	sēem	dān′ ger(ər)
kēen	nēar	trēat	wīde
bēa′vers(ər)	pēel	rēal′ ly(ē)	fur(ər)
do(ū)	ŭn′ der(ər)	äre	warm (ôr)
bēat	fēar	smăck	

Beavers

What do we see near the rocks in the pond? We see a beaver as it eats a plant. It will not see us if we are still.

A beaver may seem to be really mean. It is not mean, but it may have a fear of us if we get too near. We may hear it beat its tail on the pond with a big smack. That is the way it tells the other beavers that danger may be near.

The plant is a treat for a beaver to eat. A beaver will also peel bark and eat trees. God gave them keen teeth.

Beavers use heaps of sticks to help them make their homes on ponds. They swim under that heap of sticks to sleep. They have fur that keeps them warm. Beavers are clean and neat. God gave them wide feet so they can swim fast.

Beavers, beavers,
It is a real treat
To stay near the pond
And see you swim and eat.

Questions:

1. What do the beavers eat?
2. Is a beaver mean?
3. If a beaver has fear, what will it do?
4. Where do the beavers sleep?

WORDS TO KNOW: Study Chart 9

Jŭs′ tĭn	lēans	spēak	ōats
fēeds	lēap	hôrse	hāy
grēen	dēep	a̲(ə) frāid′	māne
swēet	rēach	chīld	sôft
crēek	ēach	kīnd / hīgh	nōse

A Big, Big Friend

What is Justin doing? Is he afraid of his big friend? Oh, no, Justin is not afraid as he feeds the horse some green grass. A horse has big teeth, so Justin takes care as he feeds it. See the horse reach for the green grass. It leans over the fence, but will not leap over it.

Justin treats the horse with the sweet grass. It also likes to eat wheat, oats, and hay. The horse's ears hear Justin speak in a kind way, and it will not be mean to him. Justin pats its soft nose.

Justin's dad may help him have a ride on the horse. The horse likes to wade in the creek. It is not deep, but it is muddy. Justin will sit high and will hold onto the horse's mane. Each child may like to have a friend like this.

Questions:

1. What did Justin feed his big friend?
2. How does Justin speak to the horse?
3. Where does the horse like to wade?

WORDS TO KNOW: Study Chart 9

crēa' ture(chər)	mēals	strông
lēap	ē' vĕn	tōad
lēaf	spĕ' cial (shəl)	touch(ŭ)
mēet	Mr. (mĭs' ter[ər])	

A Pond Friend

What is this little creature sitting on the green leaf? Meet Mr. Toad. It has no tail, but it has strong legs to help it leap. Some toads live on land. Some even live in trees. They have little feet that help them swim. They feel cold and bumpy if you touch them.

Do you think toads like to eat the same kinds of meals that you eat? Oh, no, I do not think so. They like to eat insects, but I do not like to eat insects. Do you think you would like to sleep in the same kind of bed as the toads? No, I like my neat, clean bed.

God made each little creature,
that is clear to see.
He made them very special,
which shows how great He must be.

Questions:

1. What does the toad's legs help it to do?
2. What do toads like to eat?
3. How does a toad feel if you touch it?

Do You Remember?

Peter will eat his cereal and help his mother clean the home. At three o'clock a dear friend will come to see Peter. Will it be Grandpa? Will it be Aunt Jean? No, it will be Pastor Dean.

Beavers are not mean, but they will fear us if we come near them. They have keen teeth and can peel and eat trees. God gave them wide feet so they can swim fast.

Justin's friend has big teeth and likes to eat sweet grass. The horse likes to wade in the creek. Justin is not mean to his big friend. He speaks in a kind way.

A toad is a little creature that can sit on a green leaf on the pond. It likes to eat insects. God made the toad to feel cold and bumpy.

Questions:

1. What time was Peter's dear friend coming?
2. Did Peter know what friend was coming?
3. What kind of teeth do beavers have?
4. What kind of feet do beavers have?
5. What does Justin's big friend like to eat?
6. What creature can sit on a green leaf in a pond?

Lesson 26

WORDS TO KNOW: Study Charts 10 and 14

greāt	fīnd	bird(ər)	few(yū)
ēa' gle(əl)	rē mīnd'	hurt(ər)	down(ou)
stēal	chīld	try(ī)	fo͞od
mēat	wīld	sky(ī)	thăt
bēak	mīle	eyes(īz)	trēe
pēak	pīne	răb' bĭt	clĭff
mīght	dīves(z)	pĕck	a(ə) no'(ə) ther(ər)

The Great Eagle

What kind of bird is this? It is a big, wild eagle. See it fly in the sky. It will try to find some meat to take to its nest. It will carry the meat with its big feet and claws. It will eat with its beak. Its eyes can see a rabbit or a fish from a mile up in the sky. Then it dives down to get the food. The eagle might even steal from another bird.

Only a few birds can fly as high as the eagle. It has a nest high on the peak of a cliff. Few men will go to find its nest. The eagle might fight and peck at them.

As this eagle sits in a big pine tree, it can see far up in the sky and far down on the ground.

A kind child will not hurt a bird. His mother and father will remind him that God made each bird.

Questions:

1. How far can the eagle's eyes see?
2. What might the eagle try to get and eat?
3. Where is its nest?
4. Who made each of the birds?

WORDS TO KNOW:

Study Chart 10

Al'ĭ son(ə)	pīle	whīte	break
nīce(s)	līke	brēeze	blōw'ĭng
kīte	tīght	strĭng	there(âr)
wīres(z)	tīe	wĭnd	

Flying a Kite

The day is nice and cool as Alison takes her kite outside. The breeze is just right to help her kite fly. The kite looks like it is a mile away.

Alison's father helped her make the kite from a kit. He had to tie a white string on it so it is tight. The wind is strong and might make the string break.

Alison had to run fast to get the kite up into the sky. She will try to stay away from trees and wires. The kite will not make the birds afraid. While there is a breeze, the kite will fly. It will come down in a pile if the breeze stops blowing. Do you like to fly a kite?

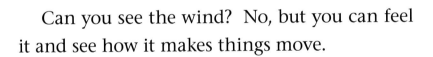

Can you see the wind? No, but you can feel it and see how it makes things move.

Questions:

1. What helps the kite to stay up in the sky?
2. What did Alison's father tie to the kite?
3. What will happen if the breeze stops blowing?

WORDS TO KNOW:			Study Chart II
Kā' tie(ē)	līne	fēel' ers(ər)	bŏt' tom(ə)
pōle	fīght	whĭs' kers(ər)	căt' fĭsh
hōld	līke	tāste	wä' ter(ər)
stōnes	hŏŏk	rĭv' er(ər)	com'(ə) ĭng
rōad	lŏŏk	down(ou)	fŭn' ny(ē)

What Is on the Line?

Hold on, Katie, hold on to your pole! The line is tight, and that means a fish is on the hook. Try to stand still and not slip on the stones. The fish might fight to get away. Dad is coming on the road. He will come and help you with the fish. The fish on Katie's line is funny to see. It has feelers that look like whiskers. It is a catfish.

A catfish likes to taste and eat a lot of things. It helps keep the water clean as it stays down near the bottom of a river. God made many kinds of funny catfish.

Dad came and helped Katie get the fish off the hook. They will not take the fish home. It will be happy to get back into the water.

Questions:

1. What kind of fish did Katie catch?
2. What funny things did it have on its face?
3. Who helped Katie get the fish off the hook?

WORDS TO KNOW: Study Chart II

Mīke	pōke	cōld	kīnd' ly(ē)
rēached(t)	spōke	strōll	ôr
frôg	hōle	shōw	tŏŏk
cōat	hōpes	pĭck	lĭve

Mike Finds a Little Frog

What is Mike holding in his hand? Yes, it is a little green frog. He hopes the frog will not leap off his hand as he stands still.

Mike had put on his coat and went for a stroll along the road. He came to a hole near a stone. He spoke kindly as he reached down to pick up the frog. He did not poke it or hurt it.

Mike can see that the frog has no tail. It has big eyes and a cold nose. God gave it webbed feet that help it to be a fast swimmer and a good jumper. It likes to live near water and land.

After he took the frog home to show his mother and father, Mike took it back to its hole. It will be best for the frog. Mike did not know what to feed it. The frog will find the right bugs to eat.

Questions:

1. What is Mike holding in his hand?
2. Where did he find the frog?
3. How did its nose feel?
4. What did Mike do after he showed the frog to his father and mother?

Do You Remember?

The eagle is a big, wild bird that has a nest high on the peak of a cliff. Its eyes can see a rabbit or fish from a mile up in the sky. The eagle might even steal from another bird.

Alison likes to fly a kite on a nice, cool day. She had to run fast to get the kite up in the sky. She will stay away from the trees and wires.

Katie has a funny catfish on the hook of her line. She stands on stones as she holds the pole. The catfish likes to live near the bottom of a river and to eat lots of things.

Mike likes the little green frog he got along the road. The frog was in a hole near a stone. It has a cold nose and likes to eat bugs.

Questions:

1. What might the eagle do to get food?
2. Where is the eagle's nest?
3. What does Alison do to make the kite fly?
4. What will she not go near with the kite?
5. On what is Katie standing?
6. Where do catfish like to be?
7. Where did Mike find the frog?
8. What does it like to eat?

WORDS TO KNOW: Study Chart 12

where(âr)	glūe	Tĕx' as(ə)	nĕ' ver(ər)	hăp' py(ē)
Nīle	few(ū)	learn(ər)	Kăn' sas(zəs)	school(k)
Jūne	new(ū)	frūit	New(ū) Yôrk	
tūbe	flew(ū)	jūice(s)	New(ū) Jer'(ər) sey	
ūsed	drew(ū)	glōbe	Mĭs sis(ə) sĭp' pi(ē)	

June Has a Globe

Where is the Nile River? Where is the Red Sea? Where is New York? Is New York near Texas? Is Texas near Kansas? How many miles are from Mississippi to New Jersey?

June likes to know many things. June may never go to these places, but she has a new globe to help her know where these places are. Last year she flew to New York with her father and mother.

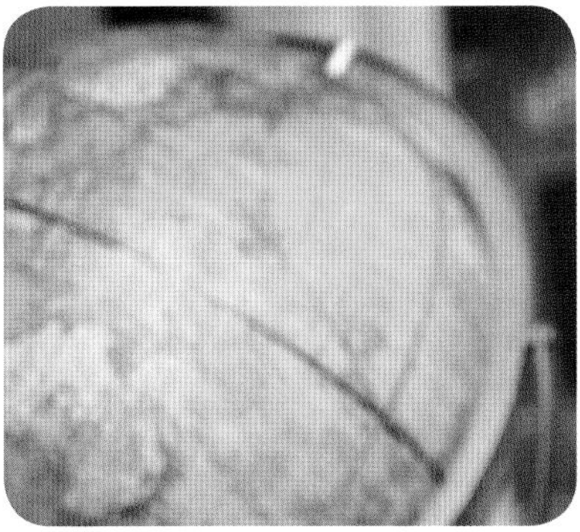

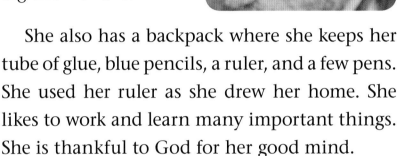

June will use her new globe as she will do her school work. It will help her see how big the world is.

She also has a backpack where she keeps her tube of glue, blue pencils, a ruler, and a few pens. She used her ruler as she drew her home. She likes to work and learn many important things. She is thankful to God for her good mind.

June is happy when it is lunchtime. Her mother packed some fruit, juice, and a sandwich.

Questions:

1. What will help June know where places are?
2. Where does she keep her pencil, pens, and glue?
3. What will June have for lunch?

WORDS TO KNOW: Study Chart 12

Bruce(s)	grew(ū)	pär' ty(ē)	gĭfts
tūne	blew(ū)	bal(ə) lo͞on'	said(ĕ)
Lūke	tā' ble(əl)	so͞on	căn' dles(əl)
Clūe	birth'(ər) dāy	ôr' ange(ĭnj)	sĭnce(s)
	out	yĕl' lōw	

Bruce's Birthday Party

Who do you see at the table? Bruce is having a birthday party. A few of his friends just sang the happy birthday tune for him. Soon they will eat the birthday cake and have a glass of fruit juice. They laughed as he blew out the candles.

Do you see the three balloons? I see an orange balloon, a blue balloon, and a yellow balloon.

Bruce is nine years old. Do you see the nine candles on his cake? His father said he grew a lot since his last birthday. He had to get some new shoes to fit his big feet.

His friends gave Bruce gifts for his birthday. Sue gave him a blue plane. June gave him a gray flute. Steve and Luke gave him a game called Clue, and Ben gave him a paint set with a brush and tubes of paint. Bruce thanks his friends for the nice gifts. They will play some games and then go home.

Questions:

1. How old is Bruce?
2. What colors are the balloons?
3. What did Steve and Luke give Bruce?
4. Would you like to have come to his party?

WORDS TO KNOW: Study Charts 15, 25a

shhh	knew(ū)	quĭck' ly(ē)	screen
Hăn' nah(ə)	brown(ou)	sôft	would
Dūke	răts	dôg	bŏx(ks)
ōld	bē hīnd'	bärk	mīce(s)
ver'(âr) y(ē)	quīte	yärd	lĕt tŭce'(s)

Hannah's Pet Rabbit

Ssshhhh! Hannah is holding her cute brown and white rabbit. It is about three years old, and it is quite big. Her friend Luke gave it to her. He knew it would be a nice pet for her.

It grew very quickly as she gave it food and water. It has long ears and soft fur, and it is in the same family as rats and mice. It is tame and not wild as some rabbits are. It sleeps in a box made of little screens. It likes to eat lettuce.

It will hop along behind Hannah as she goes for a stroll in the yard. It likes to eat the grass and leaves. It will run away if it hears a dog bark.

Hannah is very kind to her pet. Its name is Duke. Would you like to have a rabbit like this?

Come, little rabbit,
Come hop to me.
I will be very kind
As you will see.

Questions:

1. Who gave Hannah her cute rabbit?
2. Where does it sleep?
3. What will make it run away?

WORDS TO KNOW: Study Charts 6, 15

Cärl	stärt	blăck	fĕn' ces(səs)
Bär' ba(ə) ra(ə)	gär' den(ə)	chĭck' en(ə)	push(o͝o)
färm	härd	flŏck	ōb ey'(ā)
lärge(j)	pō tā' tōes	stŭck	once (wənts)
bärn	câr' rots(ə)	trŭck	grō' ce(sə) ries(ē)

Carl and Barbara

Carl and Barbara live on a farm. They have been playing in the yard near the large barn. They hear Mother calling, so Carl holds Barbara's hand as they start to run to the garden to see her. Mother will pick apples from the trees and dig up some potatoes and carrots.

Life on a farm can be so much fun for children, but it is hard work for their fathers and mothers. Carl and Barbara can help in many ways.

Carl feeds the chickens and gathers the eggs. The chickens scatter everywhere if the dog barks at them. Carl likes to ride with Father in his black truck as they go to fix fences. Once the truck got stuck in the mud. Another day they saw a flock of ducks flying high in the sky.

Barbara works with Mother in the garden or in the home. She rides with her in the car as she drives to the market. Barbara helps to push the cart as Mother puts in jars and other groceries.

Do you help your father and mother with work? Do you come as soon as they call you? A good child will always obey right away.

Questions:

1. Where was Mother when she called the children?
2. What does Carl like to ride in?
3. What does Barbara do as Mother shops?

Do You Remember?

June knows where to find the Nile River on her new globe. She likes to learn and do her school work. She is happy to eat some fruit and a sandwich for lunch.

Bruce is happy to have his friends come to his birthday party. He blew out nine candles on his birthday cake, and he grew a lot since his first birthday. The friends gave him many nice gifts.

Hannah is holding her cute rabbit that is three years old. It has long, soft ears. It is tame and sleeps in a screen box. Hannah is kind to her pet rabbit Duke.

Carl and Barbara run to see Mother in the garden as she picks apples. Carl sees the chickens scatter when they hear the dog bark. A good child will always try to obey his parents.

Questions:

1. Where does June see the Nile River?
2. What does she have for lunch?
3. Who came to Bruce's birthday party?
4. What did his friends give him?
5. How old is Duke?
6. Where does Duke sleep?
7. What was Mother picking in the garden?
8. What does a good child try to do?

WORDS TO KNOW:

Study Chart 15

Lŏn′ na(ə)	härd′ ly(ē)	cär′ pĕt	fĕtch
Chärge(j)	a(ə) pärt′	stärt′ ĭng	tēach
März	härm	fŏl′ lōws	Flôr′ i(ə) da(ə)
		a(ə) mount′	

Lonna and Charge

What a large dog Lonna holds in her arms! Charge was born in March and has grown so much! His tan fur coat feels so soft and warm. He is a quiet dog, but he will bark if he thinks harm may come to Lonna.

Lonna's family lives in Florida where it is always warm. When she is at home, Lonna and Charge are hardly ever apart. He follows her to the park. He stays close to her as she pulls weeds in the garden. He sleeps on a little carpet next to her bed. Lonna's father even allows Charge to ride in the car with the family.

Do you think that Charge eats a lot of food? You are right. He eats a large amount of food. The family buys a large carton of dog food each week.

Lonna is starting to teach Charge to obey her. He comes when she calls him. He sits and lays down when she tells him to do so. He will catch a ball and fetch a stick. He makes a big mess as he gets a bath. Lonna is thankful to God for her dear pet.

Questions:

1. In what month was Charge born?
2. Where does he like to sleep?
3. How much food does he eat each week?

Lesson 37

WORDS TO KNOW: **Study Chart 16**

owl	sound	därk	claws (ô)
fowl	ground	shärp	hoŏked(t)
how	a(ə) round′	hĕad	bēaks
ŭp′ sīde	loud	doôr	stĭnk
mouse	small (ô)	gĕn′(j) tle(əl)	

The Owl

Do you know what kind of bird this is? Yes, it is an owl. An owl is a fowl with eyes that seem very big. It may look wise and gentle, but it is not wise or gentle. If you are quiet, you may see an owl fly around.

God made many kinds and sizes of owls. They all have sharp claws and strong, hooked beaks. They are good hunters. They can see and hear very small and quiet creatures.

Most owls hunt at night when it is dark. When they fly, they do not make a loud sound. If an owl hears the quiet sound of a mouse, it will fly down to the ground and catch it. Owls eat lots of bugs. They really stink if they eat a skunk.

Have you ever seen how God made the owl's head to go way around and upside down?

If you hear the sound "who, who" at your door, do not open it. You will not want an owl in your home.

Questions:

1. Is an owl wise and gentle?
2. When do owls hunt?
3. What happens if an owl eats a skunk?

Lesson 38

WORDS TO KNOW: Study Chart 16

cows(z)	ground	shāde	môrn' ĭng
brown	mouth	lōw' ĭng	lärge
al(ə) low'	a(ə) mount'	twīce(s)	ăf ter(ər) nōōn'
found	hour	ear'(ər) ly(ē)	

The Friendly Cows

This is a hot, quiet day. The cows have found some shade under a big tree. The brown and white cow has rested on the ground. Another cow bowed down to eat some grass with her mouth. They will chew and chew on the grass for a long time.

The cows are slowly going to the barnyard. Our cows will not run away from us. They will allow us to pat them.

In about an hour, the farmer will milk the cows and give them hay and oats to eat. He must feed and milk them twice a day. He will do it early in the morning and late in the afternoon. They give him a large amount of milk. He is kind to his gentle cows.

When you drink your next glass of milk, think about the gentle cows and the farmer who helps you get this milk.

The friendly cow all red and white,
I love with all my heart;
She gives me cream with all her might,
To eat with apple-tart.
She wanders lowing here and there,
And yet she cannot stray,
All in the pleasant open air,
The pleasant light of day:

Questions:

1. Where do the cows like to be on a hot day?
2. What does one cow have in her mouth?
3. What will the cows allow the children to do?

WORDS TO KNOW: Study Chart 18a

spĕ' cial(shəl)	côr' ner(ər)	shy(ī)	pies(ē)
môrn' ĭng	sôrt	noise(z)	neigh'(ā) bôr
Jôr' dan(ə)	nôrth	pōō' dles(əlz)	al(ô) rĕad' y(ē)
doôr	môre	twĭn	a(ə) dôr' a(ə) ble(əl)
floôr	chôres	pŭp'	

Two Special Gifts

One morning Jordan could hear some noise in the barn. What was making that sound? It was not the sound of a cow or a horse. It was not the sound of a cat or an owl. He asked his father to tell him what was making the noise.

His father took him by the hand and led him behind a door. There Jordan heard the sound again. This time he knew what was making the noise. There in the corner on the floor was a bright red box. Two little faces were peeking out at him. Two adorable white puppies were ready to jump out and play.

Jordan quickly knelt down to pet them. At first they were sort of shy, but soon they began to lick Jordan on his face and run around the barn. Jordan had never had poodle puppies before. They were twin dogs that were born on the farm north of Jordan's farm. The neighbor already had two dogs, and he did not think he needed two more.

Jordan is so happy his father will let him keep them. They followed him as he did his chores and everywhere he went.

Questions:

1. Where was the red box?
2. What was in the red box?
3. Who gave the puppies to Jordan?

Do You Remember?

Lonna's tan dog Charge is soft and warm. It is large to hold in her arms. Charge can catch a ball and fetch a stick. Lonna's father will allow Charge to ride in the car.

An owl is not wise or gentle. It will use its sharp claws and strong beak as it hunts at night. God made the owl's head to turn way around and upside down.

The cows have found shade by a tree on this hot, quiet day. They chew and chew the grass in their mouth. The farmer must feed and milk his cows twice a day.

Jordan saw a red box in the corner on the floor. Two little white poodles were in the box. They followed Jordan as he did his chores.

Questions:

1. What can Charge do?
2. Where is he allowed to sit and ride?
3. What does the owl use to catch its food?
4. Who made the owl?
5. What kind of day is it for the cows?
6. How many times a day are the cows fed and milked?
7. What kind of puppies did Jordan find?
8. What do the puppies do as Jordan works?

WORDS TO KNOW:

Study Chart 18a

côrn	côrn′ fiēld	heard(ər)
tôrn	rē pôrt′	rā′ di(ē) ō
stôre	thôrns	ăn′ i(ə) mals(ə)
Fôrd	scôrch	wĭn′ ter(ər)
stôrm	pôrch	wĕath′ er(ər)
	hŭsks	

Picking Corn

Jordan's father has picked some corn. He has torn open the husks and is looking at it to see if it is ready to pick. The husks are still green, and the corn looks sweet. Mr. Ford will chop the corn and store it for his animals to eat this winter.

Mr. Ford heard a report on the radio that a storm was coming from the north. He will try to pick the corn this morning before the storm comes. It is not good to pick corn if it is wet.

Mr. Ford has worked hard to keep weeds and thorns out of the cornfield. He is glad the weather was not too hot and the sun did not scorch the corn. He is thankful that God sent good weather this year.

After he has worked he will sit on the porch and watch Jordan play with his two white poodles.

Questions:

1. When will Mr. Ford use the chopped corn?
2. What did the weather report say?
3. What will Mr. Ford do after his work is finished?

WORDS TO KNOW: Study Chart 19

Rā' chel(ə)	soup (o͞o)	does(əz)	măth
ro͞om	no͞o' dle(əl)	fôur	lĕs' sons(ə)
scho͞ol(k)	cho͞ose	proud	learn (ər)
no͞on	chĭck' en(ə)	bē găn'	grănd' fä ther(ər)
spo͞on	go͝od / bo͝ok	stär	grănd' moth(ə) er(ər)

Rachel's School

This is Rachel. Do you think that she is in a room at school? She is in school at home. Her mother and father teach the lessons to her. She likes to read, print, and learn about math. She gets a star if she does good work.

She began school when she was four years old. Now she is five and can read lots of books.

She read a book about a goose and a rooster. She also read about a child who got a new tooth. Her grandfathers and grandmothers are proud of her.

Rachel can read some of the Bible. How important it is to know how to read! It is important for a child to do good school work at home or away from home. Will you try hard to do good school work?

Soon it will be noon, and Rachel will choose to eat chicken noodle soup with a spoon. Her mother will give her some milk and fruit, too.

Questions:

1. Where is Rachel's school?
2. Who are Rachel's teachers?
3. How old was Rachel when she began school?
4. When it is noon, what will Rachel choose to eat?

Lesson 43

WORDS TO KNOW: Study Charts 19, 20

A' bi(ə) gāil	should(o͝o)	balls(ô)
wo͝ol	could(o͝o)	walls(ô)
lo͞ose	would(o͝o)	crăck' ers(ər)
mo͞od	pĭnk	bē cause'(ô)
sto͞ol	call(ô)	bă năn' a(ə)
scärf	tall(ô)	chā' sĭng

A Cool Day

The days are getting cool as it will soon be winter. Abigail has a new pink cap and scarf to keep her warm. Her grandmother made it for her with soft, wool yarn.

Abigail is in a happy mood. Jordan's mother made a call to Abigail's mother on Saturday morning. She asked if Abigail would like come and play with Jordan and his two poodles in the afternoon. Jordan's family has a large family room. It is a safe place for the puppies to play. They like to run along the walls chasing after their balls. Abigail's mother said Abigail could go.

She sat on a tall stool and had some soup and crackers at noon. She should not eat an apple because she has a loose tooth, so her mother gave her a banana. Soon the tooth will come out, and a new tooth will grow in its place.

Abigail is happy to have Jordan as her friend. They are kind to each other. Mother is now ready to take her to Jordan's home.

Questions:

1. Who made Abigail's scarf and cap for her?
2. Who will Abigail play with in the afternoon?
3. Why did she not eat an apple?
4. Are you kind to your friends?

WORDS TO KNOW:

Study Chart 14

pīne	hīgh	moun' tains(ə)	wōes
shīne	nīgh	sound' ly(ē)	joys(oiz)
whīle	līght	brĕak' fast(ə)	griēfs
smīle	sīght	pō' ĕm	wätch
pret'(ĭ) ty(ē)	quī' et(ə)	snōw	pēace'(s) ful(ə)

The Lord Is Near

While Abigail was soundly sleeping, her father and mother saw snow fall on the ground. It made everything look so clean and pretty. It fell on the pine trees and the mountains. They could see stars shine in the dark sky. It was a quiet, peaceful sight.

In the morning after Abigail had her breakfast, her father read from the Bible. Then he read this nice poem:

When the stars, at set of sun,
Watch you from on high;
When the light of morn has come,
Think the Lord is nigh.
All you do, and all you say,
He can see and hear;
When you work and when you play,
Think the Lord is near.
All your joys and griefs He knows,
Sees each smile and tear;
When to Him you tell your woes,
Know the Lord will hear.

Anonymous

Questions:

1. Who made the pretty snow to fall?
2. Who is always near us and knows all about us?

Do You Remember?

Mr. Ford will soon pick the corn. He heard a weather report on the radio about a storm. He will try to pick the corn before it gets wet in the storm. He is glad Jordan likes his poodles.

Rachel has her school in her home. Her mother and father teach her to read and learn about math. She can read many books. She is happy she can read some of the Bible, too.

Abigail is in a happy mood because she will soon play with Jordan and his poodle puppies. She sat on a tall stool and she ate her lunch. Her mother will take her to Jordan's home.

Abigail's father and mother saw snow fall to the ground while she was sleeping. After breakfast, her father read from the Bible. He also read a nice poem that says the Lord is always with us.

Questions:

1. What does Mr. Ford want to pick?
2. What will the storm do to the corn?
3. What do Rachel's parents do for her?
4. What important book can she read?
5. Is Abigail happy that she will play with Jordan?
6. Who will take her to Jordan's home?
7. What did Abigail's father and mother see as she slept?
8. Who is always with us?

WORDS TO KNOW: Study Chart 18b, 21

cōal	bē' ĭng	boil	jăck' et(ə)
Roy(oi)	point	moist	warm(ôr)
ĕn joy'(oi)	voice (s)	rĕad' y (ē)	lăst
boy(oi)	hĕad	drĭnk	rē mĕm' ber(ər)
cär' rot(ə)	wä' ter(ər)	pär' ents(ə)	

A Big Snowman

Do you think that you could hear happy voices and noise from this snowy yard? Roy and his family have made a big snowman. They have put a carrot with a point for its nose and six small lumps of coal for its happy mouth. It has sticks for its arms and two stones for its eyes. They will look for a hat for its head. They enjoy being together like this.

It is a joy to see a boy and girl enjoy being with their parents. These may be some of the best days for them to remember. God has blessed their happy home.

They will soon go into the house to warm up their hands. Mother will boil some water for a hot drink. They will take off their moist jackets and mittens and let them dry as they wait for the drink to be ready. Roy hopes the snowman will last for a long time. What will happen to it if the sun shines on it and the days get warm?

Questions:

1. Who is making the happy noise in the yard?
2. What did they use for the snowman's nose?
3. What did they use for its arms?
4. What do they do with their jackets and mittens?

Lesson 47

WORDS TO KNOW:

Study Charts 21, 26

Troy / spoil	sāfe' ty(ē)	Sā' vior(yər)	prē pâred'
hĕalth	freē' dom(ə)	peō' ple(əl)	couch
quī' et(ə)	Jē' sus(zəs)	clōthes(z)	dē lĭ' cious(shəs)

Thanksgiving Day

Everyone is quiet as Grandpa Troy prays and thanks God for all the blessings this family has had from God. This is a special day of thanksgiving, but we should be thankful every day. They are thankful for good health, for safety, for freedom in this country, for the joy of Jesus as Savior, and for the Bible.

The family enjoys being together. They do not want anything to spoil the way they are friends as a family. They remember that many people in other lands do not have as much as they do. They pray for them and send boxes of food and clothes to share with some of them.

Soon it will be time to eat the delicious food that Grandmother and Mother have prepared. They will eat more than they should, but that is what happens sometimes. Do you think Grandpa Troy may take a nap on the couch when he is finished with his meal?

Questions:

1. Who is praying for the blessings on the meal?
2. Does the family enjoy being together?
3. What may Grandpa Troy do after he eats his meal?
4. Name one thing for which they are thankful.

WORDS TO KNOW:

Study Charts 22, 23

Cŏn' nel(ə)	Sĕp tĕm' ber(ər)	first(ər)
ĕx(ks) cīte' ment(ə)	Thurs'(ərz) dāy	turn(ər)
hur'(ər) ries(ēz)	worst(ər)	curb(ər)
sĭs' ters(ər)	per'(ər) son(ə)	hurt(ər)
broth'(ə) er(ər)	swerved(ər)	bought(ô)
yoŭn' ger(ər)	per(ər) hăps'	thought'(ô) ful(ə)
	cir'(ər) cle(əl)	

A Great Snowstorm

"Wheeee!" Connel yells as he hurries down the snowy hill. He has come to sled with his family. He has five sisters and one younger brother. The sled goes so fast down the steep hill that there is much excitement. He was the first to try out the new blue sled that his sisters bought him for his birthday in September. Next it will be his sister Kelsey's turn. Connel is being kind to share his sled with his family. He is a thoughtful boy.

During the early morning on Thursday, the worst storm of the year came from the north. It was hard for a person to drive his car to work. One man's truck swerved, went in a circle, and hit a curb. He was not hurt, and he was thankful that he did not hit another person.

Perhaps the safest place on a snowy day may be on a sled on a hill.

Questions:

1. When did Connel get his sled?
2. Who had the next turn?
3. What happened to one man in his truck?

WORDS TO KNOW: Study Chart 22

to(ə) bog'(ä) gan(ə) third (ər)

Here Comes Another Sled

"Look out! Here comes Dad with Justin and Alison! Get out of their way!" yelled Mother.

The family has another sled to use. It has more room on it than Connel's sled. This sled is called a toboggan and is made out of wood. Dad is not holding on with his hands. Will he get hurt? If he does fall off, he will not get hurt, because the snow is soft.

Alison holds onto a rope and Justin holds onto his dad's knees as they go fast. The weather is cold, but they do not mind that. They are having so much fun together. This is the third time they have come down the hill. They will feel very tired when they go home. Perhaps Justin will fall asleep in the van.

Each person in our family should be our very good friend. We should be kind and thoughtful to each other. We should treat each other as we want to be treated.

Questions:

1. Who is riding on Dad's sled with him?
2. How many times have they gone down the hill?
3. How should we treat each other?

Do You Remember?

The family makes happy noises with their voices as they make a large snowman. They give it two stones for its eyes and six lumps of coal for its happy mouth.

The family is quiet as Grandpa Troy prays to God on this special Thanksgiving Day. He is so thankful for everything. The family will soon have a delicious meal.

Connel is sledding with his five sisters and little brother. His blue birthday sled goes so fast. During the early morning on Thursday, the worst storm of the year came from the north.

Dad sat on the toboggan with Justin and Alison. They came down the hill very fast. The family is kind and thoughtful to each other. They treat each other as they want others to treat them.

Questions:

1. What is the family making out of snow?
2. What did they use for the snowman's mouth?
3. On what special day is Grandpa Troy praying?
4. What will the family soon have?
5. What color is Connel's sled?
6. On what day did the storm come?
7. Who sat on the toboggan with Dad?
8. Did their sled go slow or fast?

Lesson 51

WORDS TO KNOW: Study Chart 22

fū′ture(chər)	au′(ô) tŭmn	wĭth out′
squir′(skwər) rel(ə)	ā′ côrn	bur′(âr) ied(ē)
rē turn′(ər)	scrătch	sŭp(ə) ply′(ī)

A Busy Little Squirrel

As a farmer sat under an oak tree, he saw a gray squirrel come down from another tree, scratch the ground, and return. The man could not decide what the squirrel was doing, so he went as near to the spot as he could without being seen.

Down came the little creature again with an acorn in its mouth. After putting it into the ground, the squirrel filled up the hole with soil.

One day when the winter came, the farmer was near the same spot and saw the squirrel scratching up the acorns it had buried in the autumn. This was its winter supply of food.

"If all men would take a lesson from you," said the farmer, "and be good workers as they think of the future, it would be a good thing for the world. God has made you in a special way."

The squirrels do not scratch up all the acorns they hide. Many fine oak trees have grown from acorns planted by squirrels.

Squirrels are very fond of nuts; but in the spring, when their supply of nuts is gone, they live mostly on young leaves and buds. They may also be seen eating their lunch from your bird feeders.

Questions:

1. What did the farmer see the squirrel do?
2. What did the squirrel eat in the winter?
3. What happens if the squirrel does not dig up all his acorns?

WORDS TO KNOW: Study Chart 16

lärge(j)	greāt	rā' där
līght' house	stēer	sēa' gŭll
beau'(yū) tĭ ful(ə)	crăsh	whāle
tow'(ou) er(ər)	warn(ôr)	dôl' phĭn
pow'(ou) er(ər)	dān' ger(jər)	crēa' tures(chərs)

The Lighthouse

This tall house that you can see on the large rock along the water is a lighthouse. On this beautiful evening, you can see the light with great power in its tower. At night this important light is seen far out at sea, and the men on ships can tell where to go.

If it were not for this lighthouse, the ships would crash into the rocks along the shore. Long ago this tower was very important to men in the tall ships and fishing boats. How glad they were to see that bright light in a dark night or in a storm! They would then know which way to steer their ship; and they would be sure that they could get help if they were in danger.

The ships we see today have radar that also helps to warn of danger.

How would you like to live and work in a lighthouse? You might see a white or gray seagull catch a fish with its beak. Perhaps you would even see a whale or dolphin leap from the water. Our great God made the waters to be filled with fish and many other living creatures.

Questions:

1. What kind of house do you see?
2. How does it help the men in boats and ships?
3. What do ships and boats today have to help them know where they are going?

WORDS TO KNOW: Study Chart 22

fĭn' ger(ər)	so͞oth~~e~~d	chirp'(ər) ĭng
tē~~a~~s' ĭng	Jan(ə) ĕll~~e~~'	chāng~~e~~d(j)
ĕx(ks) ăm' ple(əl)	rē' al(ə) īz~~e~~d	clōth~~e~~s
com'(ə) fort(ər)	lov'(ə) ĭng ly(ē)	lă~~u~~gh(f)
a(ə) wā' ken(ə)	dĭs turb'(ər)	young'(ə) er(ər)

Be a Good Example

The birds chirping in the big trees next to the house did not awaken the family, nor did the bright sun shining through the windows. It was a little person standing in her bed and saying, "Uh, uh." Everyone knew what she meant. Janelle thought it was time to begin the day.

As soon as her mother changed her clothes, Janelle went into her big sisters' room. She liked to follow them wherever they went. They were able to dress themselves and neatly make their beds. They knew how to keep busy all day long. But Janelle had so many things to learn.

How did she learn? She watched and did what her sisters did. If they ran, she would run. If they laughed, she would laugh.

Two little birds lived in a cage in Janelle's home. The birds were funny and noisy, but they did not like to have people poke their fingers into their cage. One day Janelle saw one of her sisters feeding them. Janelle tried to do it also. She put one of her fingers close to the cage, and the little birds pecked it.

Her sisters and mother lovingly comforted her and soothed her sore finger. She learned to never do that again. Her sisters and mother talked about what had happened. They realized that Janelle was trying to be like her sisters. Their mother told them to be careful to always obey because Janelle watches them closely and copies everything they do.

Question:

1. How should you act around younger children?

WORDS TO KNOW: Study Chart 23

Paul(ô)	caught(ô)	yawn(ô)	out sīde'
Au'(ô) drey	plowed(ou)	walked(ô,t)	
aw'(ô) ful(ə)	thaw(ô)	cough(ôf)	
thought(ô)	lawn(ô)	fall'(ô) en(ə)	

A Winter Morning

Early one Thursday morning, Paul woke up before anyone in his family. He quietly walked into the living room and looked out the front window. More snow had fallen on the lawn during the night, and everything looked beautiful and clean. It would take a long time for all that snow to thaw.

As Paul stood and looked, a snow truck came around the corner. It plowed the street, but did not plow his family's driveway. The noise did not disturb his family, and they kept on sleeping. He heard his sister Audrey cough. She had caught an awful cold, but was feeling much better.

Suddenly Paul thought about something. He saw his father's black van all covered with snow. He had better tell his father about that. It will make him late for work if he has to clean off the van and shovel the driveway. He ran into his father's room and quietly whispered in his ear. Paul's father sat up with a yawn and thanked Paul for telling him about the snow. His father said that Paul could help him with this work.

Paul quickly put on his clothes and went outside with his father. He was glad his father thought that he was big enough to help. He always likes to be with his father.

Questions:

1. Who was the first person to wake up?
2. What came by and plowed the snow?
3. What did Paul's father have to do before he went to work?

Do You Remember?

A farmer saw a gray squirrel run up and down a tree. It was burying acorns in the ground. When winter came, the farmer saw the squirrel scratching up the acorns to eat. God makes the squirrels do this.

A lighthouse is important to the people in ships and fishing boats. When it is dark, it tells them that rocks are along the shore. God made the waters to be filled with fish and many other living creatures.

Janelle was a little person who liked to follow her

sisters around. She tried to do the things they did. Her mother and sisters soothed her finger after the pet birds pecked it.

Early on Thursday morning, Paul looked out of the living room window. Beautiful snow had fallen on the lawn and on his father's black van. He was glad his father wanted him to help work in the snow.

Questions:

1. What was the squirrel first doing with the acorns?
2. Who made the squirrel to do this?
3. How does the lighthouse warn men in ships?
4. Who filled the waters with living creatures?
5. What did Janelle like to do?
6. Why did her finger hurt?
7. On what day did Paul see new snow?
8. Was he sad or glad to help his father?

Lesson 56

WORDS TO KNOW: Study Chart 22

spĕ′ cial (shəl)	wor′(ər) shĭp	ver′(ər) ses(əs)
Sŭn′ dāy	ē ter′(ər) nal(ə)	căt′ tle(əl)
hŭm′ ble(əl)	hĕav′ en(ə)	stall(ô)

A Special Morning

While Joe was sound asleep one Sunday morning, his mother gave him a gentle pat. It was time for him to wake up and get ready to go to church. He slowly opened his eyes and saw the bright sun coming through his window.

Joe's family goes to church every Sunday, but this was a special day. On this day as they worship God, they will remember the birth of the Lord Jesus.

They will read about the birth of Jesus from the Bible. It will tell them that He was born in a cattle stall. Humble shepherds were the first to hear about His birth. Joe will hear verses from the book of Luke.

It is important to learn all that we can from the Bible. It teaches that we may have eternal life in heaven if we love the Lord Jesus. The word "eternal" means it will last forever.

Let us worship and love the Lord each day by doing what He wants us to do. That means to obey Him. We learn how to obey from reading the Bible, God's Holy Word.

Questions:

1. Where was Joe's family going this morning?
2. Who were the first to hear about Jesus' birth?
3. How can we show that we love the Lord?

WORDS TO KNOW: Study Chart 17

Sā' vior(yər)	stŏŏd	Chrīst(k)	poôr
hō' ly(ē)	lōw' ly(ē)	shĕl' ter(ər)	shăll
roy' al(ə)	lāid	stā' ble(əl)	crowned
Dā' vĭd's	mān' ger(jər)	crā' dle(əl)	ŏx'(ks) en(ə)
cĭ' ty(ē)	Mâr' y(ē)	mīld	

Once in Royal David's City

Julie is in her Sunday School on the morning everyone is celebrating the birth of Jesus Christ. She is thanking God for sending His dear son.

Once in royal David's city
Stood a lowly cattle shed,
Where a mother laid her Baby
In a manger for His bed:
Mary was that mother mild,
Jesus Christ her little Child.

He came down to earth from heaven
Who is God and Lord of all,
And His shelter was a stable,
And His cradle was a stall:
With the poor, and mean, and lowly,
Lived on earth our Savior Holy.

Not in that poor lowly stable,
With the oxen standing by,
We shall see Him, but in heaven,
Set at God's right hand on high;
When like stars His children crowned
All in white shall wait around.

Cecil Frances Alexander, 1848

This may be a good song to learn by heart.

Lesson 58

WORDS TO KNOW: Review Charts 12 and 17

clōse(z)	prīze	does(ŭz)	crē ā' ted(ə)
grāin	ēach	dew(ū)	här' mo(ə) ny(ē)
plāin	drēam	guīdes(z)	
shīne	knēel	gu ärds(z)	
līfe	earth(ər)	glōw	

Who?

Who made the sun so warm and bright?
Who made the moon to shine with light?
And all the stars that glow at night?
God did.

Who made the earth to give us grain?
Who feeds it with the dew and rain?
Who made each creature on the plain?
God did.

Who gives us life and all we prize?
Who guards us when we close our eyes?
Who guides us when at morn we rise?
    God does.

Who knows each thing that, night or day,
I dream or think or do or say?
Who hears me when I kneel to pray?
    God does.

Author Unknown

When God created all the earth,
    It was His will that we
Should love our neighbor as ourselves
    And live in harmony.

Florence Hinchman

Questions:

1. What three things did God put in the sky for light?
2. Who should we thank for all that we see?
3. Who should we thank for taking care of you and me?

WORDS TO KNOW:

gône
a(ə) crôss'
lông
bē lông'
wrông
Mr. Hall (ô)

daugh'(ô) ter(ər)
taught(ô)
naugh'(ô) ty(ē)
brought (ô)
walks(ô)
talks(ô)

Review Chart 23

cook' ies(ē)
blīnd
vĭs'(z) it(ə)
līfe
a(ə) gō'
Să' tur(ər) day

Eric Visits His Neighbor

Eric has gone to see his neighbor Mr. Hall who lives with his daughter. Every Saturday morning Eric walks across the lawn to his home.

Today he brought some cookies that his mother had made. He also brought some books.

Mr. Hall is almost blind, so he cannot read. He is so happy to have Eric visit and read to him. Mr. Hall talks about his life when he was a child long ago. Eric and Mr. Hall are good friends.

Eric will read a book about a naughty dog who ran away from its home and went across a big street. The dog almost got hit by a truck. A man caught the dog and brought it back to where it belonged. The dog had to be taught that it was wrong to leave its yard.

Soon it is time for Eric to go home. Mr. Hall thanks him for coming and reading. Eric says he will come again next Saturday.

Questions:

1. Who has Eric gone to visit?
2. Why can't Mr. Hall read?
3. What is Eric doing for Mr. Hall?
4. What did the dog have to learn?

Do You Remember?

Joe's mother woke him up because it was time to get ready to go to church. On this special day they would be reading from the book of Luke in the Bible about the birth of Jesus. We should love the Lord each day and obey Him in every way.

"Once in Royal David's City"

He came down to earth from heaven
Who is God and Lord of all,
And His shelter was a stable,
And His cradle was a stall:
With the poor, and mean, and lowly,
Lived on earth our Savior Holy.

"Who?"

Who made the sun so warm and bright?
Who made the moon to shine with light?
And all the stars that glow at night?
God did.

Poem by Florence Hinchman

When God created all the earth,
It was His will that we
Should love our neighbor as ourselves
And live in harmony.

Every Saturday Eric goes to visit his neighbor Mr. Hall. Eric's mother has made some cookies for him to bring. Eric also brings a book to read to Mr. Hall because he is almost blind. Mr. Hall is so happy to have Eric as his friend.

Questions:

1. Why did Joe's mother want him to get up?
2. What book in the Bible did they read?
3. When does Eric visit Mr. Hall?
4. What does Eric bring for him to eat?

Lesson 61

WORDS TO KNOW:

com'(ə) pa(ə) ny(ē)
skīes
plēad
sĕt' tle(əl)
blāz' ĭng
won'(ə) der(ər) ĭng

Review Chart 17

frĕt
stôr' ies(ē)

Books Are Good Friends

Books are happy company
When the skies are gray.
Books are friends that never plead,
"Let's go out today."

Books are quiet company,
Glad to settle down
By a lamp and blazing fire,
Far away from town.

Books will never fret or sigh
At the window pane,
Wondering how to pass the time
When the Lord sends rain.

Friends we need and friends are good
For every special day,
But as we look inside our books
New friends and stories come our way.

Author Unknown

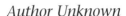

The Bible is the best book
With lessons we should know;
It tells how Jesus died for us
Because He loved us so.

Questions:

1. What would be a good friend to spend time with on a gray day?
2. What is the best book?

WORDS TO KNOW:

Study Chart 29

ăn′ i(ə) mals(ə)	ăn′ swer(ər)	Ad′(ă) am(ə)
Eve(ē)	sĕc′ ond(ə)	săng
quĕs′ tion(chən)	fĭfth	sông
di(ə) vīd′ ed(ə)	crē ā′ tion(shən)	thĭnk
fourth(ôr)	third(ər)	

Days of Creation

These students sang a song as the class began. Their Bible teacher has just asked a question. Most of the students think they know the answer. The teacher asked if anyone could tell what God created on the six days of creation.

Daniel says that on the first day God created light. Alison says that God divided the waters so that there was a sky on the second day.

Elijah says that on the third day God made the land and sea. He also created every kind of plant to grow on the land.

David tells that on the fourth day God made the sun, moon, and stars. Connel knows that on the fifth day God created the birds and fish.

Lonna says that on the sixth day God created all the animals. Best of all, He created Adam and Eve in His image. He saw that it was all good. Kelsey answers that on the seventh day God rested from His work of creation, but He never rests from caring for His work. Our God is so great!

After the class finished their lessons, they talked and played. They have become good friends and are glad they have learned so much about the Bible.

Questions:

1. On what day did God create the birds and fish?
2. On what day did He create the sun, moon, and stars?
3. What did God create on the sixth day?

WORDS TO KNOW: Review Chart 27

ĭn' ter(ər) ĕst ĭng
ĭn vĕnt'
com(ə) pū' ter(ər)
type(ī)
ĭn vĕn' tion(chən)
ma(ə) chine'(ē)
prob'(ä) lems(ə)
fū' ture(chər)
mĕm' o(ə) ry(ē)
weigh(ā)

An Interesting Machine

God has given people good minds to invent many important things. One of these inventions is called the computer. This book you are reading has been printed by a computer. This special machine can be used in many ways. When these were first made, they were very large. Now some of them do not weigh much and are so small that you can hold one in your hand.

Samuel is listening as the teacher helps him learn. The class is learning to type, work their math problems, draw pictures, and play games. They will learn much if they obey and listen to their teacher. Listening is the best way to learn.

These lessons will be helpful to them in the future. If they work for their church or a company, or study in their home, a computer can be very helpful. Can you read the poem that the children were asked to type on the computers? Can you learn to say it by memory?

God has made the wide oceans,
And God made the land,
He made each little creature you see;
All the stars in the sky
Were put there by His hand;
Best of all He made you and me.

Author Unknown

Questions:

1. What invention did God help some people to invent?
2. What is the best way to learn?
3. What did God put in the sky?
4. What was the best of His creation?

WORDS TO KNOW: Study Charts 6, 7

hock'(ä) ēy	whăck	wrông
E'(ē) than(ə)	scôre	côr rĕct'
pŭck	hĕl' met(ə)	

Ice Hockey

"All right, Ethan, here comes the puck! Keep watching it and try to hit it to the goal," said Ethan's father.

The puck slowly came toward Ethan, but then it stopped. Ethan took short steps closer to the puck and gave it a whack.

"Ooops," said his father. "That is going to the wrong goal." The other team got the puck and tried to make a score with it.

When the bell rang, Ethan and his father sat down on the ice and laughed. The teams were made up of fathers and sons having a good time playing ice hockey.

Before the teams played the last part of their game, Ethan put on his helmet and had his skates tightened. He will try to remember the correct goal this time. He will try to skate without falling so often. He will stay close to his father and learn more about the game. This was a wonderful way to spend a Saturday morning with his father and his friends.

Questions:

1. What happened when Ethan hit the puck?
2. On what day were the teams playing hockey?

Lesson 65: Review

Do You Remember?

Good books can be like good friends to us. We can enjoy learning as well as reading interesting stories. These book friends are quiet company for us, and are never sad or mad. The Bible is the best book for us to read.

The children in the Bible class learned that God created our world in six days. On the fourth day, God made the sun, moon, and stars. On the sixth day, He created all the animals. Best of all, He created Adam and Eve in His image.

God gave people good minds to help them invent many important things, such as computers. When they first made them, the computers were very large. Now some computers can be held in a person's hand.

Ethan and his father had a good time playing hockey. Most of the time, Ethan missed hitting the puck. He will stay close to his father and learn as much as he can.

Questions:

1. What will our book friends never be?
2. What was the best part of God's creation?
3. Who gave people good minds for inventing things?
4. What did Ethan and his father play?

WORDS TO KNOW:

Review Chart 26

ĭn stĕad′	cĕl′ e(ə) brāt ĭng	sŭf′ fered (ər)
dĕath	church(ər)	săl vā′ tion(shəs)
sprĭng	a(ə) dôre′	caus′(ô) ĭng
sĭn′ ners(ər)	grā′ cious(shəs)	cŏn so(ə) lā′ tion(shəs)

Good Friday

It was a pleasant evening as the family went to church. They did not mind the weather, but instead they were thankful for the spring rain. Tonight the people in their church will be celebrating the death of the Lord Jesus. The day is called Good Friday. They will sit quietly as they worship God and think about the day Jesus suffered and died for their sins. They are sad whenever they think about their sins causing Jesus such pain. Each day they ask for His forgiveness.

This is one of the songs they will sing. Do you know how to sing it?

O Jesus, we adore Thee,
Upon the cross, our King!
We bow our hearts before Thee,
Thy gracious Name we sing.
That name has brought salvation.
That Name in life our stay,
Our peace, our consolation,
When life shall fade away.

Arthur Russell, 1851

Questions:

1. What will this family think about as they worship God this evening?
2. When are they sad?

WORDS TO KNOW: Review Chart 29

vĭc' tôr	dĕc' o(ə) rā ted(ə)	pret'(ĭ) ty(ē)
wāit' ĭng	dō māin'	sāints
Chrĭs' tians(chən)	fōes	lĭl' ies(ē)
hymns(ĭ)	bē cause'(ôz)	prāised(z)
mīgh' ty(ē)	trī' ŭmph (f)	reign (ā)
grāve	rĕs(z) ur(ə) rĕc' tion(shən)	

The Day of Resurrection

Mrs. Johnson is helping her daughters make decorations for their home. This is one of the happiest days of the year! On this Sunday morning, Christians celebrate the day that Jesus arose from the grave. It is called the Day of Resurrection. Because He lives, we also will rise from the grave some day to live with Him in heaven.

Soon the Johnsons will go to church, which has been decorated with pretty lilies. The people will praise the Lord and sing hymns. This is one of the songs they sing.

Low in the grave He lay –
Jesus, my Saviour,
Waiting the coming day –
Jesus, my Lord.
Up from the grave He arose,
With a mighty triumph o'er His foes.
He arose a victor from the dark domain,
And He lives forever
With His saints to reign.
He arose! He arose!
Hallelujah! Christ arose!

Robert Lowry

How wonderful it is to have a living Savior!

Question:

1. Why is this the happiest day for Christians?

Lesson 68

WORDS TO KNOW: Study Chart 25b

Nā' than(ə)	ĕx cīte' ment(ə)	prĕ' cious(shəs)
Ab'(ă) i(ə) gāil	wāit' ĭng	cūte
fŏl' lōwed	fĭn' gers(ər)	fā' vo(ə) rīte

An Exciting Day!

What a happy day this was! The family had been praying and waiting for it to happen for such a long time! Little Nathan followed his brother and sister around in their excitement. Then his father and mother called him over to meet a special person.

"Come here, Nathan," they called. "This is

your new baby sister. Her name is Abigail. Look at her tiny fingers and toes. This is how small you were when you were born. She is a precious person just as you are. We must love and care for her. Will you help us do that?"

Nathan just looked and smiled. He had never seen such a cute, little person before. He bent over and gave her a kiss.

"She is a gift from God," said his father. "God knew about her before He created the earth. He knows and cares about everything!"

Nathan went and found his favorite blanket. He was not quite two years old, and he had a lot of things to think about now that he was a big brother. He knew his mother and father would still love him. His little sister just brought more love into their home.

Questions:

1. Whom did Nathan meet for the first time?
2. What did his little sister bring into their home?

WORDS TO KNOW: Review Charts 14, 17

pēace′(s) ful(ə) pro tĕct′ shĕp′ herd(ər)
wolf(ŭ) shĕd pro vīdes′(z)
fīght fiēlds(z)

The White Sheep

The white sheep are eating the green grass by the still water. What a peaceful sight to see them! If we are still, they might come right up to us. They are mild and will not fight with us. At night they must sleep in the shed or in a fenced place. A wild wolf might come and steal one of them. They need a person called a shepherd to protect them. The shepherd will lead them to green fields and good water. They need help in many ways.

If we love Jesus, the Bible says we are like sheep. We need Jesus to help us. He is our wonderful Shepherd. Here is a poem and song to read and learn.

I am Jesus' little lamb
Ever glad at heart I am;
For my Shepherd gently guides me,
Knows my need and well provides me,
Loves me every day the same,
Even calls me by my name.

Henrietta L. von Hayn, 1778

Questions:

1. What may happen if the sheep are not protected?
2. What is a person called who cares for sheep?
3. Who is our Shepherd?

Do You Remember?

Good Friday is a day of remembering the death of Jesus on the cross. He suffered great pain as He died for our sins. We need to thank and praise Him for doing that. We should live in a way that will honor Him.

The Day of Resurrection is a very happy day for Christians. This is when they celebrate the day Jesus arose from the grave. Because He arose, we will too.

Nathan was happy when he saw his new baby sister. She was a precious, little person. His father called her a gift from God. Nathan knew she brought more love into their family.

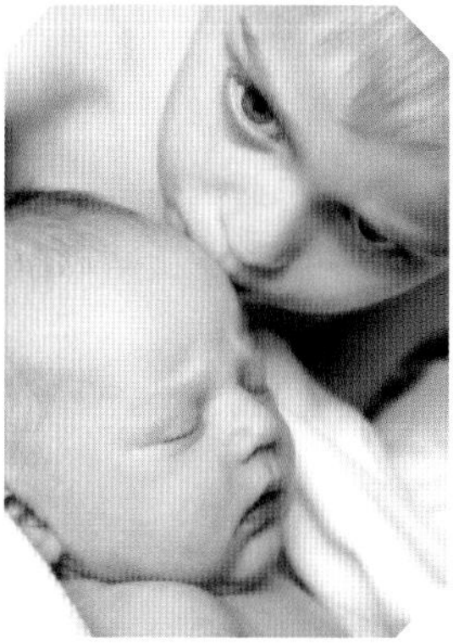

What a peaceful sight to see the white sheep eating green grass by the still water! They need a shepherd to protect and care for them. We are called sheep if we love Jesus. He is our Shepherd as He guides and provides for us.

Questions:

1. What should we do as we think of Jesus dying for us?
2. What does it mean to us to know Jesus arose from the grave?
3. What did Father call Nathan's baby sister?
4. Who protects and cares for the sheep?

WORDS TO KNOW: Review Charts 25a, b

rāce(s)	twīce(s)	vī′ o(ə) lĭn
plāce(s)	hĕl′ met(ə)	pi(ē) ăn′ ō
glănce(s)	mu(yū) sē′(z) um(ə)	tĕl′ e(ə) vĭ sion(shən)
chănce(s)	E′(ē) gypt(jĭ)	bus′(ĭz) ness(ə)

A Fast Ride

Who is coming down the road? Is he in a race? If we glance closely, we can see that it is Elijah. It is good that he remembered to wear his helmet. His father bought him his new scooter at a good sale price. Today he has his first chance to ride it in a safe place in the park near his home. The weather is nice, and he has finished his school work. He has gone down this road twice already.

Elijah has learned many things as he and his sisters and brothers study in their home. His mother has taught him how to read and work math problems. He enjoys learning about other parts of the world. His family went to a museum and saw many items from Egypt. He is thankful to God for giving him a good mind.

A good friend teaches him and his sister how to play the violin. A cousin teaches them how to play the piano. Young people can learn many important things if they work hard and do not watch many television programs. God gives each of us many hours in each day to be busy. Are you using all this time in a good way, or do you waste a lot of that time? The Bible teaches us to lead a quiet life, mind our own business, and to work with our own hands. May we try to honor the Lord in all we do.

Questions:

1. What was Elijah riding on as he came down the road?
2. Where did he learn so many things?
3. What should we try **not** to do with our time?

WORDS TO KNOW:

Review Chart 26

brĭng' ĭng	sprĕad	weigh(ā)
Căn' a(ə) da(ə)	A(ə) lăs' ka(ə)	mĕa' sure(zhər)
grāce' ful(ə)	swän	ĕx(ks) clāimed'

A Beautiful Swan

"Oh, Dad, look at that beautiful bird floating on the lake!" said Hannah.

"Yes, Hannah, that is a swan," answered Dad. "One of the most graceful birds that God made. I have read that they may grow to weigh as much as sixteen pounds. When they spread out their wings, some may measure to be about seven feet wide."

"What happens to them when the lake freezes?" asked Hannah.

"Many will fly south to the warm weather until the early spring. Then, just at the

right time, large flocks of them leave together to make the long trip back to Canada or Alaska. Sometimes the flocks may have 500 swans flying together. They live in other places, too," answered her father.

"That sure would be wonderful to see!" exclaimed Hannah. "Will her babies fly with her?"

"If the mother has been able to get an early start in building her nest and laying the eggs, the young swan should be able to fly with her."

"Oh, thank you, Dad, for bringing us on this vacation. Let's go and tell the family about the swan!" exclaimed Hannah.

Questions:

1. How heavy will some swans grow to be?
2. How wide is a swan with its wings spread out?

Lesson 73

WORDS TO KNOW: Review Charts 7 and 24

Rŏl′ lĭns	knīfe	yĕs′ ter(ər) dāy
Bâr′ ry(ē)	al′(ô) mōst	un′(ə) cle(əl)
blādes	hĭm sĕlf′	hon′(ä) est(ə)

Be Honest

As Sam Rollins was going over to his father's mill, he saw James Hall, who seemed to be looking for something.

"What are you looking for, James?" Sam asked.

"I am looking for my knife. I have lost it, and I think I lost it near this place. Yesterday when I was with Barry, we sat down here to fix our kites. Barry used it, and then I took it to cut a stick. I missed it when we were on the hill," answered James.

"Was it a good knife?" asked Sam.

"Yes," said James. "It was almost new. My uncle gave it to me last Christmas."

"Did it have a white or a black handle?"

"It had a black handle with three blades."

Sam said nothing more to James about the knife, but turned away and walked home. As he went along, he said to himself, "I think the knife I found was the one James lost. I will get it and show it to him."

He returned in a little while, bringing the knife. Holding it up to James, he said, "I found this knife where you were playing. Is it yours?"

"Yes, yes," said James, "That is my knife! Thank you so much!" Sam might have kept the knife, but he was an honest boy and knew it would be wrong.

Author Unknown

Question:

1. Why would Sam be a good friend to have?

WORDS TO KNOW: Review Charts 14, 20

nō′ tĭced(st)	grēed′ i(ə) ly(ē)
făm′ ine(ə)	quar′(kwôr) reled(ə)
lärg′(j) ĕst	pushed(ŏŏ, t)
small′(ô) ĕst	plāced(st)
mis(ə) tāke′	a(ə) mong′(ŭ)

Do Not Be Greedy

Once, when there was a great famine, a rich man called together the poor children of the town in which he lived. He told them that he would give each of them a loaf of bread each day, if they would come to his house for it.

Early the next morning, the children came to his door. When the basket of bread was brought out, each one greedily tried to get the largest loaf. They also quarreled among themselves and went away without even thanking the good man.

The man noticed one little girl waiting until the others had taken loaves and were gone.

She quietly took the last loaf, which was the smallest, and then kissed the hand of the giver to show how thankful she was. The next day the children pushed aside the smallest loaf, which was on the top of the basket, and grabbed the biggest they could find. The little girl stepped up quietly and took the smallest, thanking the man as before.

When she got home, she found some gold coins in the loaf. Thinking the man had made a mistake, she took it back to him.

"I placed the money there myself," he said, "so that you might be rewarded for being thankful. May God bless you, my dear child."

The Bible says it is God's will that we should always be thankful. Do you remember to say "thank you?"

Author Unknown

Questions:

1. How did many of the town's children act?
2. Do you like to see children act that way?
3. How did the kind man show that he was thankful for the way the little girl acted?

WORDS TO KNOW: Review Charts 17, 18b, 28

pāin	Mon'(ə) dāy	break
earn(ər)	câre' ful(ə)	lā' zy(ē)
dol'(ä) lars(ər)	joined	sor'(är) ry(ē)
mon'(ə) ēy	rē ward'(ôr)	Jŏhn' son(ə)

Never Be Lazy

James and Joe were very happy. They had a job to do. They would earn money for each hour they worked at painting a fence for Mr. Johnson.

Early Monday morning they began to work. They were careful to do good work. At ten o'clock, they took a short break to rest. When the noon fire station bell rang, they had their lunch. By three o'clock, their hands began to hurt, and it was not so much fun anymore.

"Let us ride our bikes to the store for a snack," said James. "Mr. Johnson is not at home, so he cannot see us. We will come back soon."

"No," answered Joe. "That would be wrong. He must not pay us for time we do not work. That would be taking money that we did not earn. We must finish before we ride to the store."

Most of the fence had been painted, so James joined Joe to finish the job. When Mr. Johnson came home, he was very pleased with the boys' work. He was glad that they had kept working instead of being lazy, so he gave them five extra dollars as a reward.

James was sorry he had thought about riding while they were to be working. He knew Joe was right about staying to finish the work.

Questions:

1. What job were the boys going to do?
2. What did James want to do before the job was finished?
3. How should we work when we have a job to do?

WORDS TO KNOW: Review Charts 6, 7, and 27

rē cēived′	through(ū)	ĕx(ks) cīt′ ĭng
lĕt′ ter(ər)	month(ŭ)	ĭn vīt′ ed(ə)
ĕlse	a′(ĕ) ny(ē) thĭng	grōwn
trāin	tĭck′ et(ə)	

A Letter from Grandfather

Jeff is trying hard to think about his school lessons, but he keeps remembering the letter he just received in the mail. His grandfather has invited him to come and stay on his farm for two weeks during the month of June. He just cannot think about anything else.

Will Jeff's grandfather let him do more work now that he has grown? Will his grandfather's farm dog Lad remember him? Will Jeff still remember how to ride a horse? How many chickens and ducks are there? What should he remember to pack?

Jeff has saved some money, which will help pay for a train ticket. How exciting it will be to travel through the country on a train! He has visited his grandparents' farm many times before, but he has never gone there by himself.

Jeff knows it would be wrong to not do his best in his school work. His grandfather always asks him about what he has learned. He must study now so he can talk about his lessons with his grandfather.

Questions:

1. What was Jeff thinking about as he sat in school?
2. How will he get to his grandparents' farm?
3. What will he keep doing while he is at school?

WORDS TO KNOW: Review Charts II, 25b

stā′ tion(shən)	al(ô) rĕad′ y(ē)	busi′(ĭz) y(ē)
sūit′ case	ôr′ der(ər)	pā′ per(ər)
a(ə) lärm′	bĕd′ rōōms	fī′ nal(ə) ly(ē)
lēave	drĕssed(t)	ō′ clŏck′
ĕn′ ve(ə) lōpes	grănd′ pâr ents(ə)	ĕn′ gine(jən)

Time to Leave

Rrrrring! The alarm went off at six o'clock in the morning. Jeff was already awake and dressed. Finally, the day had come when he would leave to go to his grandparents' farm.

His suitcase had been packed for two weeks, but Mrs. Smith checked to see that nothing had been forgotten. After seeing that everything was ready, she tucked in a pad of paper and some envelopes for him to write some letters home to them. She also packed a gift for Jeff to give to his grandparents.

Such a busy home! Jeff's dog barked as it followed him everywhere he went. Bedrooms were put in order. Jeff's suitcase and backpack were brought to the car.

After eating breakfast, the family prayed for a safe trip. Jeff quickly called a couple of friends to say goodbye.

"Everyone in the car!" shouted Mr. Smith. "We must be at the train station by ten o'clock."

As they got to the station, Jeff took out his ticket, hugged his parents, and got on the long train with two red engines.

Questions:

1. What time did the alarm go off?
2. Who followed Jeff around as he packed?
3. Why did his mother pack envelopes and a pad of paper?

WORDS TO KNOW:

Review Chart 20

a'(ĕ) ny(ē) môre	stŏŏd	ŭn tĭl'
hour	whĭs'tle(əl)	shī' ny(ē)
Kăn' sas(ə)	quĭck' ly(ē)	pur'(ər) ple(əl)

The Train Trip

As the train left the station, Jeff waved to his parents until he could not see them anymore. Then he settled down in his seat for a seven-hour trip to the farm in Kansas. It was interesting looking out of the window at the green countryside.

A deer stood by some water and watched as the train passed. When the train whistle sounded, the deer leaped into the woods. Jeff also looked closely as the train quickly went speeding through some small towns. He waved at the people when they waved at him.

Peeking into his backpack, he found a sandwich, an apple, juice, and some snacks. It was fun eating lunch as he traveled. Then he read a book.

Soon the sound and rocking of the train made him feel sleepy. Taking a short nap seemed to be the next thing he should do. His nap lasted two hours!

"Kansas! We have come to Kansas!" someone called. Jeff opened his eyes and saw the flat farm land. Soon the train stopped, and Jeff saw his grandfather's shiny purple pickup truck. He was very thankful for his safe trip. He quickly got ready to get off the train.

Questions:

1. What did Jeff see standing by a stream?
2. What did his mother pack for him to eat?
3. What did his grandfather drive to the train station?

WORDS TO KNOW: Review Charts 18a, b

ĕn′ ter̲ed(ər) dē lĭ′ cious(shəs) guĕss
trou′(ə) ble(əl) fôr′ ward(ər) pīēce
nŏd′ ded(ə) fĭn′ ĭsh fā′ vo(ə) rītes

At the Farm

How happy Jeff was to see his grandfather! He talked all the way back to the farm as Grandfather drove his truck and nodded his head. Lad, the faithful collie, ran to meet them. As they entered the farmhouse, delicious smells of food came from his grandmother's kitchen.

"How wonderful it is to see you!" she said as she hugged Jeff. "We have been looking forward to your visit. Tell me all about your parents and the train trip. Tell me about everything!"

"This may take a long time," said Grandfather. "Perhaps he should tell us all the news as we eat dinner."

Can you guess who was the last to finish eating his food? If you said Jeff, you are right. Before enjoying a piece of warm apple pie with ice cream, Grandfather Carl and Jeff checked on all the animals. Jeff's favorites were the cows, horses, sheep, cats, chickens and ducks. He liked them all! Grandfather Carl took very good care of each of them.

Jeff had no trouble sleeping that night.

Questions:

1. Why do you think Jeff was the last one to finish his dinner?
2. What did Jeff and his grandfather do before they ate the apple pie and ice cream?
3. Which animals did Jeff like the best?

WORDS TO KNOW: Review Chart 29

news′(ū) pā per(ər)	kĭt′ chen(ə)	brĭng′ ĭng
rōōs′ ter(ər)	chīme	front(ŭ)

Work on the Farm

"Er-er-er-er-errr!" Did Grandpa's rooster make that noise? What time is it? Where was Grandpa Carl? What good smell was coming from the kitchen? Jeff sat up and rubbed his eyes.

Hearing the clock chime five times, Jeff jumped up to get dressed and to see what was happening! Lad was just bringing in the morning newspaper from the front yard. After dropping it at Grandma's feet, the dog sat up for its treat. Then Jeff hugged Grandma good morning and ran out to the barn.

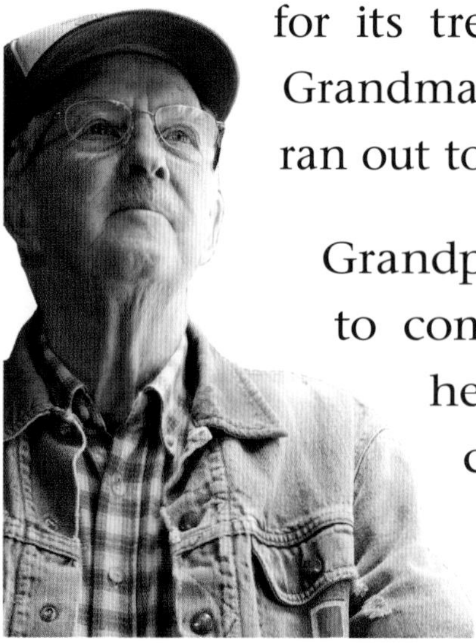

Grandpa Carl called for Jeff to come to the stable. Jeff helped Grandpa feed the cows and horses. Then they fed the chickens and ducks.

After breakfast they will have a big job to do. They need to check all the fences around the farm. But Jeff will first learn how to saddle a horse. He will be happy to ride a horse again. Nutmeg will be his horse for the next two weeks—his very own horse!

After feeding all the animals, Grandpa and Jeff walked back to the house to eat breakfast. What a day the Lord had planned for Jeff! With this much work to do, he could see why farmers had to get up early each morning.

Questions:

1. What time did Jeff wake up?
2. What would Grandpa Carl and Jeff check after breakfast?
3. How do you think they will get to the fences?

Lesson 81

Keeping Busy on the Farm

Each day Jeff and Grandpa Carl spent many hours together. There was always something to do. Grandma and Grandpa were thankful to have someone to help them with all the work.

Jeff was very careful as he came into the chicken house to gather eggs. If he came in too quickly, the chickens made such a noise and flew all around, making the air so dusty.

The sheep became Jeff's friends and came to the fence to be near him. Their wool didn't smell very good, but it was so curly and soft.

As he fed the cows, Jeff heard them make a soft, lowing sound. During his visit, the mother cat had seven black and white kittens. They would run everywhere. He could see that the ducks did not want Lad to get too close to them.

Grandpa Carl taught Jeff many things about each animal. He knew God made each one in a special way.

Of all the animals, Jeff did have a favorite one now. He spent most of the time with Nutmeg, his horse. He rode Nutmeg to help his grandpa round up the cattle, and he enjoyed taking rides after he had finished his work. He would miss Nutmeg, but Jeff knew a horse could not live with him in the city.

Jeff was so thankful for his visit to the farm of his dear grandparents. Soon he would be with his parents and telling them about his wonderful time.

Questions:

1. What do the chickens do when they are frightened?
2. What animal was Jeff's favorite?

WORDS TO KNOW: Review Chart 23

Prĕs′(z) i(ə) dĕnt
thought (ô)
pŭb′ lĭc
Wĭl′ son(ə)
sĕc′ ond(ə)
ĕx(ks) prĕs′ sion(shən)
dĭs plāy′
rĕv′ er(ər) ĕnce(s)
hăp′ pi(ē) ness(ə)

Mother's Day

Many years ago, a lady named Anne thought it would be good to have a special day to honor mothers. In the year of 1914, President Wilson said that the second Sunday in May would be Mother's Day. He asked the American people to display the flag on that day "as a public expression of our love and reverence for the mothers of our country." What a nice idea!

The Bible tells us about a wonderful woman who does what is right in God's sight. Her husband loves and trusts her. She is not lazy, but works hard all day to take care of her family. She watches over the ways of her home and buys food and clothing for her family. She also helps those who are poor. She is wise and kind when she speaks. Because she loves and obeys the Lord, her husband and children are so thankful for her.

Brad has given flowers to his mother and thanked her for her dear love and care.

Each day you should love and obey your mother. Each day you should say "thank you" for all that she does for you. Good children will try to love and obey their mothers. God will bless them with happiness.

Questions:

1. Which President said there should be a Mother's Day?
2. What should we say to our mothers every day?

WORDS TO KNOW: Review Charts 18a, b

grāve	märch	pēo' ple(əl)
Cĭv' il(ə) War(ôr)	pa(ə) rāde'	to(ū) gĕth' er(ər)
col'(ŭ) ors(ər)	fôr' ces(səs)	Mĕ môr' i(ē) al(ə)
ärmed	mu'(yū) sĭc(z)	Dĕc ôr ā' tion(shən)

Memorial Day

Memorial Day was first called Decoration Day because it was a day to decorate the graves of soldiers killed in the Civil War. Long ago in 1868, an order was given to make May 30 that special day each year.

Today people celebrate Memorial Day to remember all those who have died as they served in the armed forces of our country. People may also put flowers or a flag by the graves of friends and family members as a way to remember them.

The freedoms of our country have been paid for with a great price—the lives of many people who have fought in wars for our liberty. May we remember this and pray that our country's freedoms would not be taken from us.

Many towns will have a parade each year on this day. Bands, floats, and other people dressed in red, white, and blue will march to band music. Have you ever seen a Memorial Day parade?

Questions:

1. What did people do long ago on Decoration Day?
2. How may towns celebrate Memorial Day?

WORDS TO KNOW: Review Chart 16

plĕdge(j)
lĭb′ er(ər) ty(ē)
al(ə) lē′ giance(jənts)
bus′(ĭz) y(ē)
beau′(yū) ti(ə) ful(ə)
rē pŭb′ lĭc
jŭs′ tĭce(s)
coun′(ə) try(ē)

câre
U(ū) nī′ ted(ə) Stātes
hŏn′ or(ər)
nā′ tion(shən)
ĭn di(ə) vĭs′(z) i(ə) ble(əl)
A(ə) mer′(âr) i(ə) ca(ə)
nă′ tion(shən) al(ə)
through(ū) out′

The United States Flag

Our beautiful flag stands for liberty and many other blessings that God has given to our country to enjoy.

We should care for our flag with honor. We should pray for our country and its leaders. We should live as God wants us to live. Each day we should be thankful for our wonderful country. Have you learned this pledge?

I pledge allegiance to the flag
of the United States of America,
and to the republic
for which it stands,
one nation, under God, indivisible,
with liberty and justice for all.

Our first flag was called "the Stars and Stripes," and it was dedicated on June 14, 1777. Since 1949, our country celebrates June 14 as our National Flag Day. Our flag, also called "Old Glory," can be seen hanging in so many places throughout our country. As you hang your flag, be very careful as you handle it.

Questions:

1. What was the name of our first flag?
2. Carefully copy the Pledge of Allegiance.

A Day to Celebrate

When it is spring, we have several days to celebrate. Why do you think someone has put up their United States flag? Is it Memorial Day? Is it Flag Day? Is it Mother's Day? No, it is Father's Day. How important it is to thank our wonderful fathers for all they must do. Remember, children, to always honor your father and mother. It means that each day you should love and obey your parents, for this is pleasing to the Lord.

The Bible tells us that if a good man loves his children, he teaches, rules, and corrects them.

He should always be truthful and kind. He should comfort them or punish them as they need it. He should train them with the teachings of the Bible so they will not become unruly or disobedient.

Here is a family enjoying a beautiful Saturday morning. They have come for a walk in the field across the street from their home. Tomorrow they will go to Sunday School and church. In the afternoon, their grandfathers and grandmothers will come to celebrate Father's Day with them.

It is so nice to be in a happy family.

Questions:

1. Why was the flag put up?
2. What does a father not want his children to become?

WORDS TO KNOW: Review Chart 24

swal'(ŏ) lōw tāll — căt' er(ər) pĭl lar(ər) — Jĕn' ny(ē)

bŭt' ter(ər) fly(ī) — Bâr' ry (ē)

Enjoying Springtime

Barry, Jenny, and Mary smile as their mother takes a picture of them. This has been such a pretty day to be with their parents.

They have not been alone in this big field. They have seen some little creatures crawling among the tall grass and bushes. One of their favorites was a swallowtail butterfly. They quietly watched as it softly landed on a leaf.

What beautiful, long wings it has! The children cannot hear it make any noise. In one part of its life, it was a caterpillar. If you would have touched it as a caterpillar, it would have sent out a bad smell. That would let birds know that the swallowtail butterfly would not be a tasty snack.

It would be interesting to learn more about all the different kinds of butterflies God made.

Questions:

1. Who took the picture of the children?
2. What will happen if you touch a swallowtail butterfly when it is a caterpillar?

Lesson 87

WORDS TO KNOW: Review Chart 25a

O(ō) lĭv' ia(ēə) sprout nĭb' ble(əl)

bur'(âr) ied(ē)

A Little Sprout

"Look, Mommy," exclaimed Olivia, as she held up the little bean sprout in her hand. "My seed grew and now has green leaves. My teacher said I could bring it home and plant it outside. Where should I plant it?"

"That is very nice, Olivia. Bring it to me so I can see it," said her mother. "We will plant it near the fence and put a screen around it so a rabbit will not nibble on it. Each day you should check to see if it needs water. Won't it be interesting to watch it grow?"

God has placed into most plants little seeds that will grow into more plants. No one else but God is able to do that.

In the heart of a seed
buried deep, so deep,
A dear little plant
lay fast asleep.
"Wake!" said the sunshine,
"And creep to the light!"
"Wake!" said the voice
of the raindrops bright.
The little plant heard,
and it rose to see
What the wonderful
outside world might be.

Kate Louise Brown

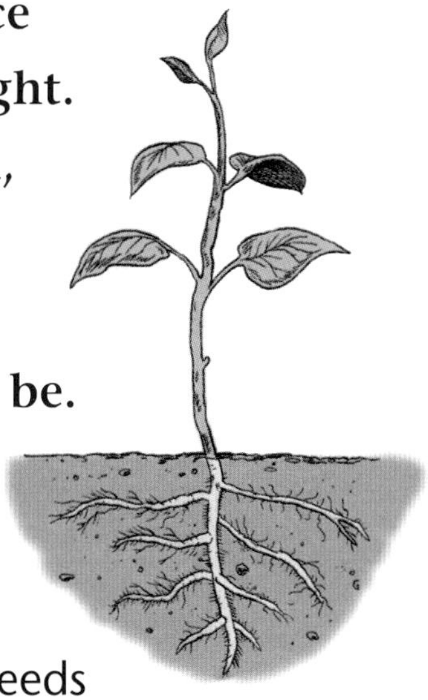

Questions:

1. Who alone makes all the seeds to grow?
2. Why should Olivia put a screen around her plant?
3. Why does a plant need water and sunshine?
4. Ask your teacher to help you name the parts of the plant above.

WORDS TO KNOW: Review Charts 7 and 25b

Al'(ă) an(ə) al(ô) though'(ō) prăc' tĭce
bāse' ball(ŏ) dĭs cour'(ər) aged(ij)

A Lesson in Baseball

"After you hit the ball, Alan, run as fast as you can to that white bag on the ground over there," said his father. "It is good we have this time to practice before we have a real game."

Alan stood at the home plate, holding the bat tightly as his father tossed the ball to him. Alan swung his bat as fast as he could, but he missed the ball.

"Try again, Son, and keep your eyes on the ball all the time," said his father.

Alan tried again to the hit the ball, but missed. Sometimes he swung too high, and sometimes he swung too low. Then, finally he hit it right to his father's feet.

"That's great, Alan! That was a good one. Let's do it again!" said his father. The two pals practiced for more than an hour before they realized it was time to go home for supper. Although Alan missed most of the time, he was not discouraged. His father told him to keep trying. Whenever a new lesson comes our way, it takes time and practice to learn how to do it.

Do you work hard as you learn new lessons?

Questions:

1. Who is teaching Alan to hit the baseball?
2. Did Alan hit the ball most of the time?
3. What should we remember when a new lesson comes our way?

WORDS TO KNOW: Review Chart 8

Au′(ô) drēy	sŭd′ den(ə) ly(ē)	mĕm′ o(ə) rīze
sprĭn′ kled(əl)	frīght′ ened(ə)	prō tĕct′

In the Garden

The morning air felt warm as Audrey sprinkled water on the family garden. It had not rained for many days, so the ground was hard and dry. The flowers smelled so sweet as she came close to them. Suddenly a little bunny ran out from under some bushes. Audrey and the bunny frightened each other. Audrey wanted to catch the bunny and keep it

in her home, but her mother told her that it would be best for the bunny to live outside.

Audrey enjoyed playing outside with her sister and brothers. She liked looking at bugs as they crawled on the trees or were found under rocks. How very interesting they were! How very special God made each one. They were so tiny, but they knew how to feed and take care of themselves, as well as protect themselves.

Audrey likes to read this poem. Can you memorize it?

All things bright and beautiful,
All creatures great and small,
All things wise and wonderful,
The Lord God made them all.
Each little flower that opens,
Each little bird that sings,
He made their glowing colors,
He made their tiny wings.

Mrs. E. F. Alexander

Question:

1. Why did Audrey need to water the flowers?

WORDS TO KNOW: Review Chart 9

I′(ī) saac(zək)	ĭn tĕl′ li(ə) gent(ə)	fī′ bers(ər)
llä′ ma(ə)	căm′ els(ə)	flēece(s)

Learning About Llamas

Isaac had never seen such interesting animals. If he stood still, these cute creatures would come over to sniff and look at him. When he touched them, their fleece felt very soft. How fun it was to watch them run and jump all around the yard, and then suddenly stop and look at him.

The farmer who owned these llamas told Isaac and his family why he enjoys raising llamas. He said that they are intelligent and want to please.

They are very gentle and friendly, and not mean. Both his eighty-year-old grandmother and six-year-old son like to pet and care for them. It is best to own a couple of llamas because they get lonely if they are by themselves.

The large llamas can be used to carry loads on their backs and pull people in carts. A pair of these llamas were in a parade, pulling a cart with four children in it.

When their fleece is sheared or cut off, it is used for spinning and weaving one of the world's finest fibers. Someday you may see a soft jacket or blanket made of llama fleece.

These animals, related to camels, usually live in South America, but now they can be found on many farms in the United States. Maybe you will be able to see a llama on a farm or in a zoo.

Questions:

1. What would the llamas do if Isaac stood still?
2. What is done with their fleece when it is sheared?
3. To what animal is the llama related?

WORDS TO KNOW: Review Chart 10

ĕx′(ks) er(ər) cīse(z)	wĕath′ er(ər)	plāy′ ground
hĕalth	ē quĭp′ ment(ə)	pŏp′ côrn

On the Playground

Do you hear any noise? Can you guess who is making it? Yes, some of your new friends are having a good time playing. They are trying to sit still on a large tire as their picture is taken.

God has blessed these children with good health. Their strong legs and arms help them run and jump, as well as hang onto the swings and climb on the playground equipment. Their skin can feel the cool weather. They can also feel if they hurt themselves.

Their ears help them hear the birds and jet planes, and when they are being called to come inside. They are thankful that their eyes help them to see each other and everything else in their lives. Their little noses are also very important to help them know what are good and bad smells. Soon they will go inside and smell a snack of popcorn waiting for them.

May each of us praise and thank God for making us in such a wonderful way.

It is important to exercise and enjoy being with friends. Do you know how to have friends? It is by being friendly to others. How enjoyable it is to play with a thoughtful, kind friend!

Questions:

1. On what are these children sitting?
2. Who made them in such a special way?

Lesson 92

WORDS TO KNOW:

Review Chart II

dĕn' tĭst	ĕx(ks) ăm' ĭne	per'(ər) ma(ə) nent(ə)
tēeth	mŭm' bled(əl)	rē plāced'(st)

A Visit to the Dentist

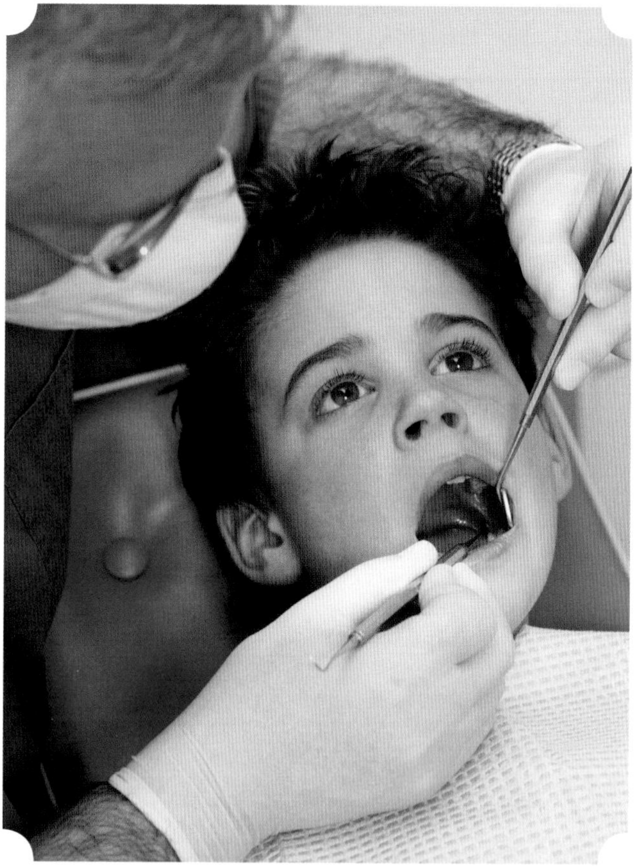

"Open wide, Daniel. Hold your mouth open wide as I check around and examine your teeth," said Dr. Fall. "Say, it looks like you are taking good care of your teeth. They look very clean."

"Uh, huh," mumbled Daniel as he shook his head up and down.

"That's good to hear. Our teeth are so important to us. We need to care for them each day in the right way," said Dr. Fall.

Daniel has already lost a couple of his first teeth, called baby teeth. When he gets older and has had all his bigger teeth, he will have thirty-two permanent teeth in all. If he takes good care of them, eats good food, and does not bang them on something hard, they will last for many years.

How important teeth are to us as we chew our food! How important they are in helping us to speak clearly! Our God did not forget about anything as He made plans for our lives.

Questions:

1. What are our first teeth called?
2. How many permanent teeth do people usually have?
3. In what two ways do our teeth help us?

WORDS TO KNOW: Review Charts 12 and 21

Grāc̲e̸(s)	rē cī′ ta̲l(ə)	hăm′ me̲r̲s(ər)
mĕn′ t̲i̲o̲n̲s(shən)	prăc′ ti̲c̲(əs) ĭng	I̲t′(ĭ) a̲(ə) ly̸(ē)

Learning to Play the Piano

Grace has taken lessons for one year and is practicing to play in a recital this evening. Her teacher is helping her as she reviews her song. She does not yet know all of the eighty-eight keys on the piano, but she can play songs using both of her hands.

If she keeps practicing each day, she might become a good pianist. There are so many songs to learn and enjoy. She is also thankful that her ears help her to know when she strikes a wrong key. At first she plays very slowly as she learns the correct notes in a new song.

Her teacher told her that the first piano was made in Italy almost 300 years ago. Many changes have been made since those early years, when a piano had only forty keys. If you looked inside a piano, you would see many steel strings. Little hammers covered with cloth hit the strings to make the sounds.

Good music is so pleasant to hear. It should be a part of everyone's life. The Bible mentions the word "music" more than 140 times. Be careful to listen to nice sounding music.

Questions:

1. How many keys does Grace's piano have?
2. How do Grace's ears help her?
3. Where was the first piano made?

WORDS TO KNOW: Review Chart 29

Mă~~t~~′ thew(ū)	sto′(ŭ) mach(ək)	sŭd′ den(ə) ly(ē)
brănch′ es(əs)	ŭn der(ər) nē~~a~~th	crē~~a~~′ ture(chər)

A Time to Play

Matthew is having so much fun. Aunt Jane has come to visit. She is the best for pushing smaller people on swings. Matthew likes to swing higher and higher. Sometimes it seems his feet might kick the branches of the tree, but they never do.

"Faster, please," he asks Aunt Jane. Aunt Jane gives the biggest push of all. A funny little feeling jumps into Matthew's stomach. He thinks maybe he would like to slow down for a while. He stops moving his legs and just watches the ground go back and forth below him.

Suddenly, in the dirt, Matthew sees a very little fellow. This tiny creature is working very hard. It is a little ant. It is trying to tug a big piece of sandwich that Matthew dropped at his picnic lunch. How will the ant ever carry such a load?

Here comes some help! Four more ants come running along. Together they can do it. God made ants to be hard workers. Now Matthew is ready to swing again, but where is Aunt Jane? She is waiting behind him with a surprise. Swish! Aunt Jane pushes Matthew up high and runs out underneath the swing.

Now Matthew is really going fast. He swings high above the ants, high above Aunt Jane, and high into the leaves. His stomach does not feel funny now. He is having too much fun. How many things God has given Matthew to enjoy!

Questions:

1. Who is helping Matthew swing?
2. What are the ants trying to carry?
3. Who gives Matthew fun things to do and see outside?

WORDS TO KNOW:

fī' nal(ə)
fā' vo(ə) rĭte
ĕs pĕ' cial(shəl) ly(ē)

Review Charts 19, 26, and 28

dĭs' tance(tənts)
ĕx(ks) prĕs' sion(shən)

The Book Is Finished!

The students have come to the final lesson. It has taken them a long time to read the whole book, but they have enjoyed meeting some new friends in the stories. The teacher asked them to tell her which was their favorite story.

Annie said she liked the story about the poor little girl and the bread. She was glad the kind man had put a coin in the smallest loaf for her.

Micah liked reading about Jeff's visit to his grandparents' farm. He especially enjoyed thinking about riding a horse like Nutmeg.

Cory's favorite story was about the two little birds that pecked at Janelle. The same thing happened to her one day when she visited her cousin's home.

Ava and Titus liked the story of the two little poodles. They have pet dogs, but they think it would be fun to have a couple of little poodles.

All the children have become good readers. It always helps us to be better readers if we read a story a couple of times. Now they can read from the Bible and many other interesting books. The children have learned to have good expression as they read, and each one holds the book just the right distance from his face. Best of all, they now enjoy reading.

Questions:

1. What was Annie's favorite story?
2. What did Micah like to think about?
3. What would Ava and Titus like to have?

God's Gifts

by Hannah McHugh

From mighty eagles to the little frogs,
From hunting owls to the friendly dogs;
All animals we find on earth below
Give praises to the God each child should know.

The ground we play on and the sky we see
Hold many gifts that we enjoy for free.
While there is still much to explore and do
Learning new things is still more fun with two.

Our pals who like to talk and play with us
And share their toys and time without a fuss
Are very special and are gifts from God
Who loves us more than seas are deep and broad!

We must be kind and fair to everyone,
And do our best until our work is done.
If we are nice to boys and girls we greet
Who knows how many dear new friends we'll meet!

Word Charts

Practice reading these **Word Charts**, which contain many of the words of the various vowel sounds. This will help strengthen your reading.

If you study each of the words on these charts, you should know about 1,400 words. May the study and completion of this reader help you to enjoy reading and make you eager to learn more from good books.

Word Charts 1 and 2

Short Vowel Rule: When there is one vowel in a word, either at the beginning or between two consonants, it usually has the short vowel sound.

Chart 1—a as in ax

Lesson 1		Lesson 2		Lessons 3 and 4	
ax	Dan	gas	plant	nap	bad
fax	fan	pass	and	sap	dad
tax	man	bag	band	tap	had
wax	pan	lag	hand	clap	lad
bat	ran	nag	land	slap	mad
cat	tan	rag	sand	am	pad
fat	van	sag	brand	ham	sad
hat	cab	tag	grand	jam	glad
mat	tab	wag	stand	lamb	camp
pat	lab	brag	cap	Pam	damp
rat	nab	drag	gap	ram	lamp
sat	as	flag	lap	Sam	ramp
can	has	ant	map	yam	stamp

Chart 2—e as in elephant

Lessons 6 and 8			Lessons 7 and 9		
Ben	web	sled	fell	let	hem
den	pep	best	hell	met	stem
hen	step	jest	Nell	net	bent
men	steps	nest	sell	pet	dent
pen	bed	pest	tell	set	rent
ten	fed	rest	well	wet	sent
egg	led	test	spell	mess	tent
beg	red	vest	bet	bless	vent
leg	Jed	west	get	dress	went
peg	Ted	bell	jet	press	spent

Chart 3—i as in **insects**

Lesson 11			Lesson 12		
bit	fig	rim	crib	dim	pill
fit	pig	Tim	fib	him	sill
hit	twig	bin	rib	rim	will
kit	wig	pin	milk	bill	quill
mitt	did	sin	silk	fill	still
pit	hid	tin	fist	hill	is
sit	lid	win	list	kill	his
big	dim	spin	mist	mill	kiss
dig	him	bib	twist	till	miss

Chart 4—**o** as in **otter**

Lesson 13					
God	dot	pot	rob	top	on
nod	got	rot	sob	crop	Don
pod	hot	tot	hop	drop	ox
flop	box	rod	jot	blot	mop
sod	lot	cob	pop	mom	fox
Tom	pox	cot	not	mob	stop

Chart 5—**u** as in **up**

Lesson 14					
bun	rut	dug	suds	hump	hum
fun	us	hug	cub	jump	mum
gun	bus	jug	club	lump	yum
run	fuss	mug	hub	mumps	dull
sun	muss	rug	rub	pump	gull
but	cuff	tug	tub	stump	cup
cut	muff	plug	stub	clump	pup
hut	puff	bud	bump	bum	fuzz
nut	bug	mud	dump	gum	buzz

Word Charts 6 and 7

Short vowel words ending with a **k** sound are spelled with **ck**.

Chart 6

Lessons 34, 64, and 76					
back	crack	wreck	brick	lock	crock
jack	quack	speck	click	rock	knock
lack	shack	kick	quick	sock	duck
pack	track	lick	stick	tock	luck
rack	beck	pick	prick	block	cluck
sack	deck	sick	trick	clock	tuck
tack	neck	tick	cock	flock	truck
black	peck	wick	dock	stock	stuck

Chart 7—Consonant Digraphs

Lessons 64, 73, 76, and 88					
shack	chap	that	thin	whip	Phil
shock	chip	than	thick	which	phase
shed	chop	them	thank	whim	phrase
shell	check	then	think	when	phone
shelf	chick	the	thumb	whisper	photo
ship	chuck	this	bath	whisker	phony
shop	chess	those	math	whale	graph
shot	chin	they	path	wheel	digraph
shut	chip	mother	with		
ash	rich	father			
cash	much	brother			
dash	such	gather			
clash	ranch	together			
hash	bench	bother			
rash	inch	lather			
mesh	pinch	weather			
rush	lunch				
brush	bunch				

Long Vowel Rule (1): When a word has ***two*** vowels, usually the first vowel says its name, and the second vowel is silent.

Chart 8

Lessons 16, 18, and 89			Lessons 17, 19, and 89		
rail	main	lame	mate	made	play
sail	pain	name	rate	fade	hay
tail	rain	tame	bake	wade	jay
fail	vain	same	cake	grade	lay
hail	brain	blame	fake	pale	may
jail	train	lane	lake	sale	pay
mail	wait	mane	make	tale	ray
nail	bait	pane	rake	stale	say
pail	ape	vane	sake	faint	way
vail	cape	ate	take	paint	pray
quail	tape	date	wake	saint	gray
trail	came	gate	flake	wave	tray
frail	fame	hate	quake	save	clay
gain	game	late		bay	stay
				day	stray

Chart 9

Lessons 21, 23, and 90			Lessons 22, 24, and 90			
bee	dear	meet	green	sheep	zeal	key
wee	fear	greet	screen	steep	feel	seem
tree	gear	beat	bean	heap	heel	beam
flee	hear	heat	dean	leap	peel	seam
glee	near	meat	lean	reap	beef	team
three	rear	seat	mean	deal	leaf	steam
sea	tear	treat	deep	heal	deed	meek
tea	clear	wheat	peep	meal	heed	peek
flea	spear	seen	weep	real	feed	seek
plea	beet	keen	creep	seal	weed	creek
ear	feet	teen	sleep	veal	greed	weak

Chart 10

Lessons 26, 27, and 91					
bite	dive	dine	wire	by	sly
kite	five	fine	wipe	my	shy
site	hive	line	pipe	cry	sky
white	hide	mine	ripe	dry	spy
die	ride	pine	file	fly	sty
pie	side	vine	mile	fry	why
time	tide	wine	pile	try	
dime	wide	fire	tile		
lime	bride	hire	Nile		
chime		tire	smile		
			while		

Chart 11

Lessons 28, 29, 77, and 92					
boat	tone	foam	poke	boast	crow
coat	zone	roam	woke	roast	grow
goat	stone	hole	yoke	toast	blow
moat	hope	mole	smoke	globe	flow
note	rope	pole	spoke	hoe	glow
vote	hose	stole	choke	toe	slow
quote	nose	coal	soak	bow	snow
wrote	rose	cove	code	low	show
bone	pose	dove	rode	mow	know
cone	dome	stove	toad	row	
lone	home	joke	road	tow	

Chart 12

Lessons 31, 32, 58, and 93						
fruit	mule	clue	tune	dew	pew	crew
suit	rule	due	prune	few	blew	grew
cute	cube	glue	use	hew	flew	screw
flute	tube	dune	fuse	Jew	slew	threw
mute	blue	June	Luke	new	chew	knew

Long Vowel Rule (2): If a word has ***one*** vowel and it comes at the end of the word, the vowel usually has a long vowel sound.

Chart 13

Lessons 4 and 11					
be	me	go	no	ho	Exceptions are **do** and **to**
he	we	lo	so	yo-yo	

The vowels **i** and **o** may have the long vowel sound when followed by two or more consonants. In this list, the letters **gh** are silent.

Chart 14

Lessons 26, 44, 69, and 74					
mild	blind	might	old	sold	molt
wild	grind	night	bold	scold	roll
child	remind	right	cold	host	toll
bind	behind	sight	fold	most	stroll
hind	high	tight	gold	post	scroll
find	nigh	bright	hold	colt	
mind	fight	flight	mold	bolt	
wind	light		told	jolt	

Words with the **ar** sound as in **arm**.

Chart 15

Lessons 33, 34, 36, and 45					
ark	arm	bar	barber	carton	sharp
bark	farm	car	art	cartoon	large
dark	harm	far	cart	card	barge
hark	charm	gar	dart	hard	charge
lark	alarm	jar	part	yard	market
mark	arch	mar	tart	lard	pardon
park	march	par	start	hardly	farmer
spark	barn	tar	chart	harp	guard
sparkle	yarn	star	garden	carp	

Words with **ow** and **ou** sound as in **cow**.

Chart 16

Lessons 37, 38, and 84		Lessons 52 and 84		
cow	down	out	mouse	mouth
bow	town	pout	house	south
how	gown	shout	blouse	ounce
now	brown	snout	grouse	bounce
pow	crown	sprout	bound	pounce
wow	clown	doubt	found	thousand
plow	frown	scout	hound	fountain
allow	tower	about	mound	mountain
owl	power	our	pound	ouch
fowl	flower	hour	round	pouch
growl	shower	flour	sound	couch
towel	coward	loud	ground	crouch
vowel	powder	proud	flounder	count
crowd	chowder			amount

Words having the short sound of **u** made by the letter **o**.

Chart 17

Lessons 57, 58, 61, 69, and 75			
son	of(əv)	brother	oven
ton	dove	another	Monday
won	love	color	nothing
done	glove	come	something
none	shove	some	tongue
month	other	from	among
money	mother	front	blood
		wonder	flood

Words with the **or** sound as in **corn**.

Chart 18a

Lessons 39, 41, 79, and 83				
Lord	sore	scorn	north	torch
cord	tore	thorn	port	porch
Ford	wore	corner	fort	scorch
or	snore	dorm	sort	orchard
for	store	storm	short	organ
door	shore	fork	sport	ornament
floor	horn	cork	report	orange
horse	born	pork	order	orphan
core	corn	stork	border	Jordan
more	torn	forth	force	

Words with **or** sound made by **ar** as in **war**.

Chart 18b

Lessons 46, 58, 75, 79, and 83			
war	warp	ward	reward
warm	wart	warn	warning

Words with the **oo** sound as in **moon**.

Chart 19

Lessons 42, 43, and 95				
moon	cool	hoot	tooth	goose
loon	pool	root	booth	loose
noon	spool	toot	roof	moose
soon	stool	shoot	hoof	choose
spoon	school	room	proof	doodle
boost	balloon	loom	coop	noodle
roost	too	boom	hoop	poodle
rooster	moo	broom	loop	pooch
tool	zoo	groom	stoop	food
fool	boot	smooth	snoop	mood

Word Charts 20, 21, and 22

Words with the **oo**, **u**, **o**, and **ou** sound as in **book**.

Chart 20

Lessons 43, 74, and 78				
book	brook	wood	put	wolf
cook	crook	woodpile	bush	wolves
hook	shook	woodpecker	push	could
look	cookies	stood	pull	would
nook	good	foot	bull	should
took	hood	soot	full	

Words having **oi** and **oy** sound as in **oil** and **boy**.

Chart 21

Lessons 46, 47, and 93					
oil	toil	joint	choice	joy	royal
boil	broil	point	hoist	toy	loyal
coil	spoil	void	moist	Roy	royalty
foil	coin	avoid	noise	enjoy	Floyd
soil	join	voice	boy	Joyce	Lloyd

Words with the **er**, **ir**, **ur**, **ear**, and **(w)or** sound as in **girl**.

Chart 22

Lessons 48, 49, and 51			Lessons 53 and 56	
father	sir	church	turtle	pearl
mother	fir	fur	hurry	worship
brother	girl	purse	sure	word
sister	bird	nurse	furniture	worm
verse	dirt	turn	furnace	world
person	first	burn	turkey	worse
herd	firm	churn	during	worst
eternal	squirrel	curb	Thursday	worth
serve	third	curl	Saturday	work
derby	circle	hurt	earn	worker
fern	circus	burst	learn	working
jerk	disturb	curtain	earth	worthless
germ	thirsty	purple	early	worthy
rooster	birthday	injure	heard	worry

Words with the **o**, **al**, **au**, **aw**, **augh**, and **ough** sound as in **dog**.

Chart 23

Lessons 48, 54, 59, and 82				
dog	along	saucer	raw	awful
fog	belong	faucet	law	awkward
log	all	haul	draw	awesome
frog	ball	auto	gnaw	caught
boss	call	pause	thaw	taught
toss	fall	cause	straw	daughter
moss	hall	because	dawn	naughty
across	tall	sausage	fawn	haughty
cloth	mall	laundry	lawn	
moth	wall	autumn	yawn	ought
gone	small	Paul	drawn	bought
long	stall	Saul	awning	fought
tongs	walk	jaw	crawl	brought
song	talk	paw	shawl	thought
wrong	chalk	saw	sprawl	cough (f)
strong				

There are ***eight*** spellings for the sound of **ar** as in **square**.

Chart 24

Lessons 73 and 86					
are	**are**	**arr**	**air**	**err**	**ear**
bare	aware	carrot	air	berry	bear
care	beware	carry	fair	ferry	pear
dare	blare	marry	hair	merry	tear
fare	flare	Barry	pair	cherry	wear
hare	share	Harry	stair	errand	swear
mare	snare	Larry	chair	error	
pare	spare	barrel	dairy	**eir**	**ere**
rare	stare	parrot		their	where
ware	square			heir	there

Word Charts 25a, 25b, and 26

C usually has the sound of **s**, and **g** usually has the sound of **j** when **c** and **j** are followed by the vowels **e**, **i**, or **y**.

Chart 25a

Lessons 33, 71, and 87	
Soft sound of c = s	
ice	race
dice	space
lice	trace
nice	fence
mice	bounce
rice	pencil
spice	city
twice	cymbals
vice	prince
ounce	lettuce
brace	celery
face	necklace
grace	chance
lace	glance
place	circle

Chart 25b

Lessons 68, 71, 77, and 88	
Soft sound of g = j	
age	wedge
cage	hedge
gage	pledge
page	engine
rage	giraffe
stage	hinge
wage	danger
large	giant
barge	orange
charge	badge
gem	manger
bridge	range
gym	change
gypsy	vegetable
Egypt	gingerbread

The vowels **ea** may have the short sound of **e** as in **head**.

Chart 26

Lessons 47, 66, 72, and 95			
head	dread	health	sweater
lead	thread	wealth	peasant
read	threaten	weapons	pleasant
dead	steady	breakfast	cleanser
death	sweat	feather	instead
bread	breath	leather	headache
meant	spread	weather	treasure
		Heather	measure

Vowels **ei** and **ey** can have the long sound of **a** as in **obey**.

Chart 27

Lessons 39, 45, 63, and 76			
eight	neighs	veil	they
weigh	freight	vein	obey
weight	neighbor		survey
sleigh	reign		prey

Vowels **ea** can have the long sound of **a** as in **break**.

Chart 28

Lessons 75 and 95		
break	steak	great

Words ending with **ng** and **nk**

Chart 29

Lessons 62, 67, 80, and 94				
bang	wing	bank	blink	bunk
gang	fling	blank	clink	chunk
hang	sling	clank	drink	dunk
rang	swing	drank	link	flunk
sang	thing	Hank	mink	hunk
tang	spring	plank	pink	junk
	string	rank	rink	plunk
bing		sank	sink	sunk
bring	flung	tank	think	stunk
ding	hung	yank	wink	
king	lung			
ping	rung			
ring	sung			
sing	stung			

Build Your Christian School Curriculum
with *DISCOUNT BOOKS*
from *Christian Liberty Press*

A FULL LINE OF SUBJECTS ...

- PHONICS
- READING
- HANDWRITING
- SPELLING
- GRAMMAR
- MATHEMATICS
- BIBLE
- CHRISTIAN BIOGRAPHIES
- HISTORY
- SCIENCE
- GOVERNMENT
- ECONOMICS

... FROM KINDERGARTEN THROUGH 12TH GRADE

AT DISCOUNT PRICES!!!

Featuring books from *Christian Liberty Press* plus *selected* titles from A Beka, Bob Jones, Christian Schools International, Modern Curriculum Press, and several other publishers.

FOR YOUR FREE CATALOG:
PHONE: (800) 832-2741

or you may write:

Christian Liberty Press
502 West Euclid Avenue
Arlington Heights, IL 60004

or you may contact us on the Internet:
www.christianlibertypress.com